I0074298

THE MANUFACTURER'S
GUIDE
to
AMAZON

THE MANUFACTURER'S GUIDE

to

AMAZON

How to Grow Your Top and Bottom Line, Beat the Competition, and Future-Proof Your Company

NATE FRIEDMAN

Mantaro Partners LLC
Seattle, WA

This book is for informational purposes only. It is not intended to serve as a substitute for professional advice. The author and publisher specifically disclaim any and all liability arising directly or indirectly from the use of any information contained in this book. A professional should be consulted regarding your specific situation.

The Manufacturer's Guide to Amazon copyright © 2023 by Nate Friedman

All rights reserved. No part of this book may be used or reproduced in any manner whatsoever without written permission of the publisher, except in the case of brief quotations embodied in critical articles or reviews.

Mantaro Partners LLC
600 1st Ave Ste 102 PMB 2276
Seattle, WA 98104
www.mantaropartners.com
Send feedback to info@mantaropartners.com

Publisher's Cataloging-In-Publication Data

Names: Friedman, Nate, author.
Title: The manufacturer's guide to Amazon : how to grow your top and bottom line, beat the competition, and future-proof your company / Nate Friedman.
Description: Seattle, WA : Mantaro Partners LLC, [2023] | Includes bibliographical references.
Identifiers: ISBN: 979-8-9891782-1-6 (hardcover) | 979-8-9891782-0-9 (softcover) | 979-8-9891782-2-3 (ebook) | 979-8-9891782-3-0 (audiobook)
Subjects: LCSH: Amazon.com (Firm) | Electronic commerce. | Selling. | Internet marketing.
Classification: LCC: HF5548.32 .F75 2023 | DDC: 658.872--dc23

Special discounts for bulk sales are available.
Please contact info@mantaropartners.com.

This book is dedicated to the memory of Bill Grdanski, who passed away on April 4, 2023. He was a dear friend of over twenty years and the founder of Mantaro Partners. His desire to help manufacturers be successful was the inspiration for this book.

Contents

Tell Me What You Think

Let other readers know what you thought of *The Manufacturer's Guide to Amazon*. Please write an honest review for this book on your favorite online bookshop.

★ ★ ★ ★ ★

PREFACE

WHO THIS BOOK IS FOR . . . AND ISN'T!

This book is written specifically to help manufacturers become successful on Amazon. If you are not a manufacturer, then this book may not be for you.

This book teaches you how to use your existing competitive advantages in manufacturing and customer knowledge to develop a sustainable e-commerce moat on Amazon and then off. Amazon can grow sales in the short and medium term, and in the long term, Amazon can strengthen your company overall, prepare you for market changes, and ensure that you will hand off a stronger company to the next generation.

This book was written to help established manufacturers understand the benefits of Amazon and how to incorporate it into their business.

I started my career in manufacturing and believe that America is built on manufacturing. Globalization has been a huge challenge that destroyed many good companies over the last fifty years. I want manufacturers to thrive in the next challenge—the world of e-commerce—and this book outlines how to do that.

I have tailored the content and the action steps specifically for manufacturers. This means that this book is *not* for the following:

- *Start-ups or companies with limited sales:* Launching an unknown product and brand is very different from being an established manufacturer with existing customers and market-tested quality product lines.

- *Direct to consumer (DTC) and e-commerce companies:* The typical DTC/e-commerce company has different core competencies than the typical manufacturer.

Additionally, you need to be a manufacturing company that can execute, improve, and invest. This book charts a simple path for you to be successful on Amazon and to develop new customers there. But it is work. Amazon is not just a new customer—it is a new opportunity. And to capture a new opportunity, you need to put in the work.

The Manufacturer's Guide to Amazon describes and details the exact work you need to do to achieve a strong presence on Amazon. I also explain common pitfalls so that you can avoid costly mistakes and teach you how to develop an Amazon go-to-market plan that gets you the highest return in a sustainable way for your operations.

AN INVITATION

ASK ME ANYTHING!

Bringing the power of the world's largest online store can change everything for you and your business. I wrote this book to share exactly how—and to guide you to more sales, more profit, and fewer headaches.

I appreciate you placing your trust in me and for taking some of your valuable time to read this book. As a thank-you for that trust, I want to offer you a free thirty-minute consulting call.

This is not a sales call or an introduction to what we do. The purpose of the conversation is to help you successfully implement the advice in this book. The call can be used to answer questions, help you solve a problem, cover a topic in more detail, or determine a high-level plan for your business. I want you to be successful in your Amazon journey, so the goal of the call is completely up to you.

Go to www.mantaropartners.com/meet to see my calendar and schedule today.

CHAPTER 1

DOMINATE OR DIE: THE CHOICE EVERY MANUFACTURER HAS TO MAKE

It All Starts with Your End Customers

Somewhere in the world is your perfect customer. Maybe that's a business, or maybe that's a person. You don't know them, and they don't know you. They may have heard of your brand or your products, but they may not know where to buy them. The one thing they do know is that they have a problem they need to fix. Urgently.

If you were in front of them giving your sales pitch, you'd make their day. Your products are exactly what they need. They wouldn't even ask the price; they would simply thank you for taking their money.

But you're not in front of them. This means they need to find a way to solve their problem on their own. So they go to Amazon.com and start searching. If they have a particular brand in mind, they might type that in, but more likely they conduct a generic search for the solution they're looking for:

- "clean a sofa"
- "kids educational toys"
- "new puppy accessories"

What will they find in the results? Will they see your products, the perfect solution to their problem, at the top of the page? Are your products even on the page? Are your products even available on Amazon? Or will your otherwise perfect customer instead find your top competitor? Somebody else with beautiful product photos, numerous positive reviews, and a price worthy of the quality?

What will your perfect customer buy?

The answer isn't up to luck. It's not even a question of which is the best product or the absolute cheapest. In many cases, the brand that wins on Amazon and that gets the majority of sales from an organic search is the brand that understands Amazon the best.

How do I know this?

My firm, Mantaro Partners, has helped manufacturers sell over $400 million in products on Amazon since 2015. Mantaro Partners is an Amazon e-commerce consulting company that helps manufacturers build fast-growing businesses on Amazon. We do this by creating a customized plan that leverages Amazon's growth engine and takes into account the manufacturer's unique strengths.

We have deep Amazon experience across multiple industries and have worked with manufacturers at every stage—from never selling on Amazon to established eight-figure accounts—and with manufacturers of every size—from family-owned businesses to public companies.

You might think that Amazon is primarily a retailer for consumer products like books, toys, and household goods. That's certainly how they started, but it's not where they are today or where they're headed.

Think of Amazon as the world's most efficient supply chain that moves any and every type of product from the factory to the end user. Those products can be anything from $0.99 commodity products to highly specialized $10,000 pieces of industrial equipment. We've sold everything under the sun on Amazon as well as things you wouldn't even imagine.

Amazon Is Changing How Customers and Markets Buy Products

For better or worse, Amazon is leading all these changes in how business is done. Amazon works directly to increase competition in every market. They view competition as a way to reduce costs to end users and increase selection.

They're reinventing distribution, turning themselves into the most efficient channel to move a given product from its source to the end user.

Amazon is ruthlessly conscious of price and goes so far as to sell products at a loss in order to be competitive. They've trained your customers to expect unbelievable deals with immediate shipping and free returns.

These trends will continue and become painful to businesses that don't adapt. Buyers will become even *more* price sensitive and *less* loyal than they already are, and companies will need to work harder to retain long-term customers.

Markets Are Evolving to Be More Direct

The internet and globalization are both making selling more dynamic and eroding the traditional structure of markets. Competition has increased, and barriers to entry into your market are getting lower and lower.

You likely see the signs in your market. And you may see the signs in your business. Maybe your sales are slowing. There's more competition than ever, and you need to work harder to keep the business you have, much less generate more.

Your distribution channels may not be as effective as they used to be either. Nothing beats a live sales expert who knows your product inside and out. But that's expensive from a hiring and retention perspective and doesn't scale. And customers don't always have time to meet with a knowledgeable sales rep—assuming they want to meet with your rep at all.

In many cases, the relationships with customers and suppliers don't matter as much as they used to.

Another unique challenge to distribution is that there are often layers between you, the manufacturer, and the ultimate end user. You make the product and then sell it to your customers, who then sell it again. And they may not even be the ones interacting with the ultimate users.

All these layers between you and the people who use your product make it harder to respond to the market quickly. The layers place you at risk of being outcompeted by a company that can react faster or that is closer to the end user. With the internet, smart companies can do exactly that—cut through those layers of distribution, interact directly with end users, and steal your market share. Unless you do something about it and get closer to your end customer yourself.

These trends will continue.

E-commerce is the solution. But you may not have a clear sense of how to implement an e-commerce strategy. Or maybe you have a strategy, but you can't hire the talent to implement it. Even worse, maybe you've already executed your strategy, and there's no measurable return on investment.

Is Your E-Commerce Strategy Missing the Most Important Component?

I talk to many companies about how they can use e-commerce to get closer to their end customers, increase sales, and grow profits in their businesses. I am always amazed by the number of e-commerce plans that were signed off on at the C-level that are nothing more than a bunch of buzzwords, outdated concepts, and expensive tactics that do nothing for the top or bottom line.

Some industrial companies have entire e-commerce departments that spend fortunes doing nothing more than creating Instagram posts and blog articles and SEO plans. They measure their results in likes and eye-balls and number of posts. These are vanity, meaningless metrics.

A real e-commerce strategy drives sales. It drives incremental profit. It opens new markets. It improves operations and brings you closer to your customers and end users. It makes your company stronger.

I know this sounds like a big endeavor. What do you do? You might be feeling tempted to just sit and wait. To continue to do business as usual. At least then you're not chasing moving targets and spending great sums of money on unproven strategies. Perhaps your current business is still profitable, so you feel that you can always catch up when the path is clearer and you have more resources.

Wrong.

The fundamental nature of business in our time is change. The increased competition, fickle customers, and evolving distribution models are destroying the old ways of work. Companies that do not cross the chasm from the past into the future will fall. Companies that can thrive in the new environment will rise above established businesses. Winners in the new business model will have lower costs, better service, and vastly superior market reach simply because they saw the future and leaped after it.

If you wait, then in the best-case scenario, you'll pay five to ten times as much to catch up later. In 2020, we completed an analysis for a large home products manufacturer that white labeled several well-known brands you would recognize in big-box stores. Although this company made the product, they did so for other companies that owned the custom-er-facing brand. As a manufacturer, they had tight margins.

The companies that owned the brands often had margins two or three times larger than the company that actually made the products. It doesn't quite seem fair that the manufacturer made less than the compa-nies that simply owned the brand and distributed the products. But this is not uncommon.

The manufacturer wanted us to look at what it would take to sell on Amazon. They were interested in developing their own customer-facing brands in order to claim a larger slice of the profit pie.

The analysis revealed a huge market—Amazon sells upward of $1 billion per year in their segment. Our client knew the market very well and wasn't so surprised by that.

What was more interesting and more surprising was the cost for them to become a leader in the market. The top three players had an average of four years as bestsellers on Amazon. That gave these brands a competitive advantage—a natural high position in the search results. The only way to attack their moat would be to invest heavily in advertising and promotions. So we estimated the investment needed to get into the top three in two years. It was a significant but justifiable sum.

Unfortunately for them, the client didn't move forward with Amazon. They came to us during COVID-19, as they were having issues keeping up with production demand for existing customers. Although it's hard to balance current and new opportunities, the cost of inaction is huge. They've missed out on a tremendous amount of sales (at higher margins) in a huge market that is getting bigger every year.

On top of that, the cost to develop their sales on Amazon has gone up. There are more competitors, and they are spending more money on advertising and promotions to develop their markets. They would have to spend more than double what they would have just three years ago.

That's the cost of waiting. The incumbent's moat surrounding their place at the top of Amazon search results becomes wider and deeper every year. Unless they make an unforced error, their advantage on Amazon will soon become financially insurmountable. And we'll have to tell this manufacturer, "Sorry. You waited too long."

This same company exemplifies another risk of ignoring e-commerce and Amazon altogether. As I said, their operations focus was on manufacturing; they're undeniably excellent. Whenever companies have approached them to manufacture on behalf of their own retail brands, they're happy to. As these retail brands grew, the manufacturer was even happier—because they sold more.

Then it all changed. Various retailers decided to bring manufacturing in-house. They used the manufacturer to build the business and then abandoned them once they reached critical mass to develop their own manufacturing capabilities. The manufacturer has since lost a huge chunk of business. On top of that, they directly developed competitors, one of which is now the number one bestselling brand in the United States. This is not the fate of every manufacturer. Around the same time we started working with another manufacturer in the home improvement space. They had a similar business model—they were a leading manufacturer for other companies' brands. Their products are sold in major brick-and-mortar stores under very recognizable brand names. They were concerned and rightfully so about solely manufacturing products that would not grant them a lasting competitive advantage.

It was the same exact story—but with a very different ending. This manufacturer was smart and decided to launch products under their own brands. Although their goal was to have their products available everywhere, they launched their brands on Amazon. They recognized that Amazon was a huge market with a low cost of entry. You can launch an entire catalog of products immediately on a reasonable budget with a short payback period.

Their products were a hit, and their initial success on Amazon helped them expand to other brick-and-mortar channels. They now have a multimillion-dollar business growing at over 40 percent a year with several bestsellers in all their categories.

The lesson here is that the rewards are great, but the risks of inaction are greater.

Most companies I meet with to discuss expansion on Amazon take the wait-and-see approach, unfortunately. They're entrenched in the way they've always done things. And so it seems too difficult to do anything different. Yet that may be the one and only decision that could save their business altogether.

Here's another example. We work with a leading manufacturer that makes products for the metal industry, where they are a well-known brand synonymous with high quality. They are a heritage brand that has been around for over one hundred years.

Amazon has been making steady inroads into more and more industries and markets, but the manufacturer never noticed. While they focused on their historical customers and distributors, Amazon grew steadily in their market and now sells to thousands of their metal industry customers a month.

One person who did notice this development was a crafty entrepreneur based out of Southern California. He started a company to white label products from factories in China and Taiwan.

He sold his products exclusively on Amazon. They were not professional quality, but they were good enough for the weekend warrior/DIYer. And with the lower overhead and cheaper sourcing, he was able to sell the products for less. At the end of the day, his products offered reasonable value at a lower price.

Because he knew how to sell on Amazon, this small entrepreneur's products quickly became bestsellers in metal industry categories. By the time he got on our company's radar, he wasn't just a guy selling out of his garage. He was a real company and selling significantly more on Amazon than the industry-leading manufacturer. The three-year-old upstart was beating the company with more than one hundred years of industry experience.

That initial success on Amazon allowed the upstart to begin selling higher-quality products. They expanded their sales from just Amazon into more traditional markets. They went from a small Amazon-only brand to competing head-to-head with the largest company in their category—competing (and winning) not just in Amazon but in all sales channels.

Thankfully, this story has a happy ending. We helped the company launch a value line of products with unique benefits on Amazon and beat back the upstart. But it took a lot of work to outcompete them. It would have been easier if, like the upstart, they followed the tactics in this book and dominated Amazon early.

All these anecdotes illustrate a simple yet stark reality: if you don't sell on Amazon, you will get left behind.

You may even go out of business given enough time.

Just listing products for sale on Amazon is not enough. You need to list your products correctly and then develop the channel for long-term success.

Just like listing your products is not enough to jump-start your sales, listing your products incorrectly can *permanently* ruin your product's sales on the platform.

We've had more than one prospective client reach out to hire us, and we were forced to turn them away because of mistakes made early in their relationship with Amazon. One in particular stands out, a company that sells fasteners (fasteners are things like screws, bolts, and the like and are a large market on Amazon), because it was so preventable.

I'll tell you that story. But first, some quick background. Selling on Amazon has a steep learning curve. To help with that, Amazon offers select manufacturers onboarding programs. This prospective client, the fastener manufacturer, took advantage of one of these programs back in 2014, initially had great success, then saw everything fall apart. They didn't know why orders stopped all of a sudden or why they weren't getting paid by Amazon for previously placed orders. So they brought in Mantaro to figure it out.

It didn't take us long to find the issue—their product pages were created with the wrong UPCs. When Amazon scanned the barcode on a case of one hundred fasteners, they considered the case a single unit rather than one hundred sellable units. So the manufacturer would send in one hundred items expecting to be paid for one hundred items, but Amazon would only receive one and pay for one.

What was surprising is that Amazon had assisted them with the creation of the listing pages and caused the error. They didn't understand how the manufacturer's products were packaged and the impact it would have on Amazon's systems. It wasn't found immediately because someone at Amazon had been manually correcting the mistake.

As soon as Amazon stopped doing that, the delicate system broke. But it was unfixable from Amazon's side due to new internal policies and procedures. This mistake caused the fastener company to give up on Amazon for good. The fastener market is now well over $100 million a year. They had the right products and pricing to be a major player in that market.

The downsides to getting it wrong on Amazon are as dangerous to a business as the upsides of getting it right are positive. The stakes are high. And the Amazon game is not optional.

Every Manufacturer Needs to Do Amazon . . . and Do It Right

Every manufacturer must have an Amazon strategy. It boils down to two primary reasons: opportunity and survival.

First, Amazon represents the biggest long-term opportunity for growth in your market. The market is huge and is growing every day. Amazon accounts for around 40 percent of all e-commerce. They sold $220 billion in products in 2022 and are six times the size of their next largest competitor (Walmart.com). Amazon is growing more than 10 percent each year.

In short, Amazon is e-commerce. The opportunity is massive and is only getting bigger.

Additionally, ignoring the opportunity puts your survival at risk. Amazon's growth primarily comes from stealing shares from traditional channels. And that's the second reason—virtually all retail sales continue to shift from old legacy channels to Amazon. Amazon is a must-have, not a nice-to-have. Each year, they onboard millions of new products and dozens of product categories. They are actively attacking your traditional channels and courting your customers and end users.

If you don't focus on that today, you are yielding your future market to your Amazon-savvy competition. This is a matter of survival for your business. If you wait too long, you could be leaving your kids a horse-and-buggy business in the age of automobiles. That's not what I want for you.

I wrote this book so that you know exactly how to win on Amazon. I want you to get your fair share of the rapidly growing pie of Amazon. I believe you have a right to win in the marketplace, and this book details the steps to take and the levers to pull to make that happen.

But the benefits to a successful Amazon seller go beyond increased sales. Winning with Amazon will make your company stronger by bringing you closer to your customers, opening new markets, and improving your ability to service your customers. Partnering with Amazon does come with challenges, but by rising to meet them, you will become a more competitive, stronger business.

Active selling on Amazon also benefits your end users. They are likely already searching Amazon for your products and want to buy them there. An e-commerce associate of ours in the art space has built a large email list of customers that they use to launch new products. Each launch email contains links to the product on both their well-known .com website and Amazon. Over half of their customers, people already familiar with their brand, still choose to buy newly launched products from Amazon over their brand.com website.

We will show you how to make Amazon your virtual salesperson—a salesperson who never sleeps and who can talk to over three hundred million potential customers.

How I Can Help You Grow Your Sales Faster Than Anyone Else

I started my Amazon journey back in 2014. At the time I bought a small e-commerce store that sold work boots.

What's funny is that I didn't know the first thing about e-commerce when I bought the business. I purchased it because it was the least user-friendly web store I had ever seen. The colors were garish, and the product photos were small and grainy. It was slow and looked like it came out of 1998. It was dated and clunky. Despite that, it made the owner a decent amount of money.

Although I didn't know e-commerce, I did know technology and how to build websites. I spent the first couple of months learning the products and upgrading the website technology to a modern platform. The launch was successful and doubled the business overnight.

That initial boost was thrilling, but sales leveled out at the new higher level after the relaunch. I was interested in growing more, and that's when I started to consider Amazon.

At that time, I didn't know how to sell to or on Amazon; I was just a customer. I liked their selection, pricing, and fast shipping. I didn't have any clue how big the market was or how to sell or if it would even be worth my while.

Family and friends discouraged me from pursuing Amazon. After all, I'd only owned the business for a few months. It was doing well, and certainly there was a lot more I could do to grow it. They were concerned that Amazon would just be a distraction. They also argued that I could always circle back in the future once things settled down.

I decided to give Amazon a shot against everyone else's judgment. It turned out to be one of the best decisions for that business, as it quickly became a multimillion-dollar channel. This was great not only from a revenue perspective but also the increased scale allowed me to lower costs. I was able to negotiate better pricing with my suppliers and be more efficient operationally. So Amazon made my company more profitable, even with sales not on Amazon.

Since then, Mantaro Partners and I have been able to help dozens of businesses succeed on Amazon. We've launched existing brands on Amazon and launched Amazon-only brands. We've doubled and tripled the growth of already successful Amazon businesses and made failing Amazon businesses successful. We've worked with manufacturers of all sizes and delivered outsized results they didn't think were possible.

Here are sales from one of our clients before and after we started working with them:

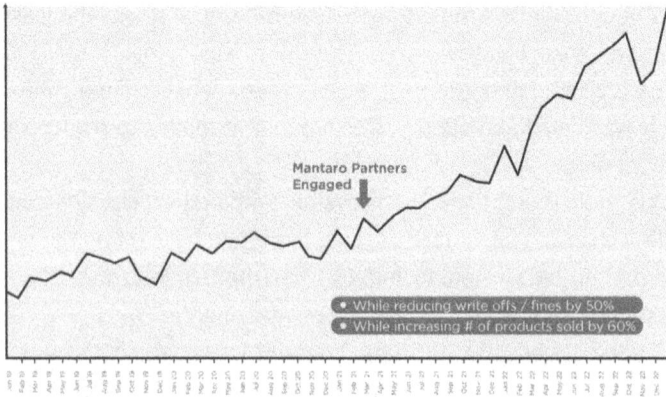

Their sales were roughly flat for several years, then after we were engaged, their sales quickly increased times two. As of the publication of this book, their growth hasn't shown signs of slowing. These results are typical, and we have clients who exceed this level of performance. If you have good products, a good plan, and a team that can execute, you should expect strong results like this.

These results are typical, but this client in particular can give us additional insights into the power of Amazon. They are a fast-growing, publicly traded company, so we have access to their overall sales and can compare their Amazon performance against their other sales channels. During the time period of this chart, they grew an average of 15 percent year over year. The flat Amazon sales did not keep up with their company growth. After engaging with us, their annualized Amazon growth is more than 65 percent, which is several times more than their overall company growth. We turned a lagging channel into one that is growing four times faster than their business overall.

What we did for them isn't magic. Over the years, we developed a step-by-step system to turn a company with no or a failing Amazon presence into a successful and highly profitable Amazon business. Our business is manufacturing successful businesses on Amazon. This book guides you through that process.

These results might sound a little too good to be true, given the fierce competition. But consider this: Amazon e-commerce grows more than 10 percent each year. If your Amazon business is not growing at least that fast there, you aren't keeping up.

Although some markets on Amazon are growing faster than others, if you are not at least achieving average, it's worth taking a closer look at what's going on. And do you really want to settle for average? We'd target two times that at least—20 percent *minimum* growth is what you should expect for year-over-year sales on Amazon.

To achieve that, there is a bit of a learning curve. That's to be expected. It just means the returns you can expect from pursuing the Amazon opportunity may be outsized.

Companies come to us either when they are new to Amazon or when what they have been doing isn't working. For companies in this stage,

Amazon is truly a growth opportunity. In many cases, you get 50 percent or even 100 percent or more year-over-year growth as we fix problems and the brand starts to get its fair share of the existing market.

When companies engage with Amazon, growth is often small at first. It takes some time for things to scale. Assuming they do the right groundwork (and follow the steps in this book), growth will begin to pick up dramatically. As we said, during the growth phase, it's possible to have multiple years of greater than 50 percent growth. But over time, as you saturate the market and capture more and more of the opportunities, growth will begin to slow down. Depending on the company and the market, this could be anywhere from two to six years. Eventually their growth will converge to the growth of Amazon's market overall:

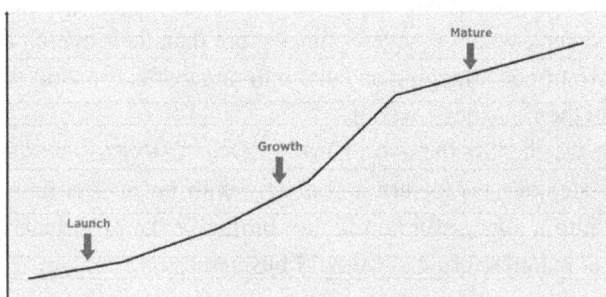

As you can see, you should be able to achieve several years of spectacular growth before settling for a sustained 10+ percent year-over-year growth on a huge slice of a huge pie. You get rewarded when you do things right on Amazon.

The best part is that you win on Amazon and you win in e-commerce. Amazon is the most demanding, highest return on investment (ROI) e-commerce channel out there. When your products win there, you'll have the formula to win everywhere.

An added benefit is that the success you get on Amazon will drive additional success off Amazon. One small example is that any marketing materials developed for Amazon can be applied to your other e-commerce channels. But the new capabilities you develop in operations, cost control, new markets, and new product development have the potential to drive sales and profit off Amazon as well.

There are some markets and product categories where the market size on Amazon may still be small today. The immediate sales potential may not be able to make it a top ten account for you. Although the potential may be small today, the growth and focus Amazon has on expansion ensures that the market expands substantially in the future. This book, effectively your Amazon playbook, is a cost-effective way to invest in the emerging market today so that you can dominate it once it becomes substantial.

Companies that follow our Amazon advice develop a moat around their products and their brand. Although Amazon has the ability for unlimited products, the practical search result space is very limited. First movers and smart movers who follow the steps here can dominate the search result real estate, thus ensuring their sales as the market grows.

Whether you hire a company to help you or you do it on your own, the time to actively develop your presence on Amazon is *now*.

You may still be skeptical, and it makes sense to be. I have made many claims, and how do you know that Amazon is the breakthrough you've been looking for, maybe the one you've been seeking for years now?

To know for sure, we first present an objective overview of the opportunity. We need the truth of the matter—and what's *not* true. With any new business opportunity, there will be myths, misconceptions, and outright lies that will doom even your best efforts. So before you learn how Amazon works for manufacturers, we first need to cover how it doesn't.

CHAPTER 2

MYTHS MANUFACTURERS BELIEVE ABOUT AMAZON THAT GUARANTEE THEIR BUSINESS WILL DIE SLOWLY AND PAINFULLY

Dan was the vice president of sales at a global industrial electronics company. He was referred to me by a client, and the only thing I knew going in was that his company had an existing presence on Amazon. He had asked for a call with me to talk about Amazon.

Dan got right to the point. "No offense, but I kind of hate Amazon. I mean, I like them personally, but from a business perspective, they just cause problems."

He isn't wrong. Amazon does cause problems for traditional selling channels.

He continued. "They're really aggressive with their go-to-market strategies and pricing. I don't think they add a lot of value to products, and they cause a lot of trouble in the market."

He was certainly feeling pain. Calls like this are fairly common as people seek expertise when things are not going as planned. Amazon requires work, and that work feels painful if you don't get good outcomes.

I wanted to explore this some more and asked, "I know you sell on Amazon. What is it exactly that is causing you problems?"

He explained how he had around two dozen national accounts on top of hundreds of smaller accounts. His sales processes and tactics worked great across all of them—except Amazon. He recognized that selling on Amazon was unique, and he was frustrated trying to put a square peg through a round hole.

"We actually cut them off last month. We've been getting so many charge-backs and fines, and they're so difficult that it was just too many headaches." He shared his sales numbers, and they were insignificant in his category and to his company. "It was just not worth it."

I asked if he knew how much his competitors were selling on Amazon. Most people I speak to have no idea of the size of their market on Amazon, so I was really surprised when he estimated that his top four competitors each brought in midseven figures. He had hired a market research firm to estimate their sales. (In chapter 4, we explain how to do this for free.)

His competitors were doing ten to thirty times his sales on Amazon! Dan then asked, "How are they getting those sales? Are they just selling to opportunistic buyers?" He was genuinely confused about why anyone would buy industrial products on Amazon when they could purchase the same products from established industrial suppliers and distributors.

Although Dan didn't understand who was buying his competitors' products on Amazon, he knew he wanted a piece of that market and that what he was doing wasn't working. But before I could give him a plan to turn his Amazon business around, I needed to first address some common misconceptions that were preventing his business from achieving its full potential on Amazon.

I share Dan's story because it captures several common misconceptions that manufacturers often have about Amazon. Addressing the most common myths and misconceptions now and learning the truth will open the door to being able to objectively understand the full potential of Amazon in your business.

Falsehood #1: "Amazon Is Just Another Sales Channel."

"Amazon is optional"—this is the foundational excuse manufacturers believe that lets them off the hook from taking Amazon seriously in their business strategy. This misconception comes in many varieties, ranging from hatred ("I hate Amazon.") to denial ("We won't sell to Amazon.") to irrelevance ("No one buys our products on Amazon.") to indifference ("We let our resellers worry about Amazon."). In Dan's case, he made it clear that he didn't like Amazon. Specifically, he didn't like how Amazon drove down retail prices (in his opinion) and compressed margins for his other resellers. (In chapter 6, we discuss why neither of these is true). But deep down he knew Amazon was not optional. That's why he called me.

Amazon is not optional because ignoring it is a threat to the survival of your business. Do not underestimate how disruptive it can be to your business today. If you engage with Amazon, the upside is tremendous. But if you ignore it, your business will die.

Look at it from the perspective of Porter's five forces, a classic framework that analyzes how competitive forces shape a market. In this case, we'll specifically analyze the impact of Amazon on your market.

Competitive Rivalry: *How intense is competition in your marketplace?*

Amazon deliberately increases competition as much as possible on their website. They do this by trying to list every product and by having the best search that connects buyers with sellers. They actively encourage price wars and ruthlessly match the prices of other retailers (online and brick and mortar). As a result, they are the biggest, most efficient, and most brutal marketplaces in the world.

New Entrants: *How easy is it for new entrants to enter the market?*

Amazon has dramatically reduced the cost for new entrants to connect to potential customers. It has never been easier for a business to copy your bestselling product, put it online, and connect directly with your customers.

Power of Suppliers: *How much power do your upstream suppliers have over you and your competition?*
Your supplier market has its own set of pressures. Amazon arguably has the same negative impact on your supply chain as it does on your market. This would reduce the power that suppliers have in raising your prices.

Power of Customers: *How much influence do customers have over your pricing and business?*
Amazon strives to be the most customer-centric company and makes empowering customers central to everything they do. They do this in several ways:

- Encourages customers to be more price sensitive by increasing price transparency
- Makes returning easy and implicitly allows a try-before-you-buy option with no-questions-asked return policies
- Introduces customers to new and alternative brands and promotes high-quality no-name brands
- Trains customers to be impatient by expecting fast and free shipping
- Gives customers a large voice with product reviews that ruthlessly summarize product quality (sometimes unfairly)

All these Amazon strategies dramatically increase the power of customers on the website and have trained customers to expect similar experiences on other websites and with other retailers. After all, why would someone buy from Retailer X when Amazon offers fast, free shipping and no-questions-asked free returns. Retailer X must match that or they will bleed customers.

The impact Amazon has on manufacturers' customers is similar no matter how you sell to them. Customer expectations are increasing, and their tendency to switch channels and brands is increasing as well. You need to work harder to keep your customers.

Power of Substitutes: *How can products from different industries impact your business?*

The classic example is the streaming services that are killing cable TV. To understand how Amazon is increasing the power of substitutes, you first need to understand how people search on Amazon. When people search for products on Amazon, they are really searching for solutions. People want to "clean my garage floor," "get rid of the poison ivy in my yard," or "hang a picture of my family on the wall," and they search for solutions to these problems. They may have a product in mind, but their primary goal is buying a solution, not a product.

Amazon has gotten really good at connecting buyers to solutions. You might manufacture the most potent degreaser, the best herbicide, or the highest-quality nails. Amazon knows buyers don't care and will gladly pick a competitor or even a substitute that may not even be on your radar.

To summarize, Amazon is weakening historical competitive advantages and hurting your legacy markets. This is true for every product-based market. Some markets are already impacted more than others, but it's safe to say that all these trends will continue and grow.

The only question is what you're going to do about it. You have two choices—ignore the trends or acknowledge and leverage them.

Ignoring will inevitably lead to more pain. Eventually these forces will drive you out of business as your more savvy competitors evolve to embrace (or at least deal with) them.

Or you can leverage them. In fact, these trends can be opportunities. Imagine that you have embraced e-commerce and have fully integrated Amazon as a customer. Your product pages communicate your right to win in the market. Because you're leveraging the trends outlined in Porter's model, your products are the bestsellers on Amazon because they are the best option in your market. You are stealing share from your competitors and developing new adjacent markets. And imagine that this increased volume helps you plan your utilization better and gives you more negotiating power with suppliers. This book will show you how to use Amazon to create this long-term growth and to build a strong company in the process.

Falsehood #2: "Amazon Will Eat Up My Existing Sales."

This is what Dan assumed. He knew his competitors were selling millions of dollars each in products on Amazon. He thought the person buying on Amazon was the same one who normally bought from other channels.

From his perspective, the primary drivers for why his customers bought his products on Amazon were pricing and fast shipping. If Amazon had a deal, or the customer needed it delivered tomorrow, they bought from Amazon. Otherwise they'd buy the same product from a more traditional channel.

In his mind, it was largely a zero-sum game. His company, or more likely his competitor's company, would get the sale regardless—because he assumed the customer was simply exercising a preference between buying through their traditional industrial channels or through Amazon. Either way, the same brand and the same company get the sale.

Although it is true that buyers on Amazon shop for specific products and choose Amazon for convenience and value reasons, we have found that the Amazon customer is very different from the customer in other channels. The Amazon customer can be a new, untapped buyer.

This is often very eye-opening for clients. We work with a large tool manufacturer with significant sales on and off Amazon. Amazon is a top five account for them. Despite its noteworthy size, only 26 percent of their company bestsellers are bestsellers on Amazon. Seventy-four percent of their top Amazon sellers are not considered top sellers off Amazon.

Industrial Brand X we represent with around 1000 skus
#1 on Amazon is #96 off Amazon
#3 off Amazon is #145 on Amazon

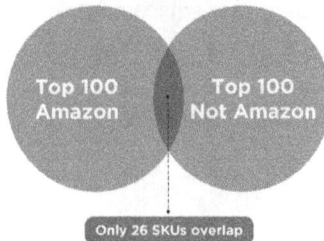

Top 100 Amazon

Top 100 Not Amazon

Only 26 SKUs overlap

These results are typical. In all likelihood, your Amazon market and customers will be different from your existing market and customers. Amazon grows your pie. There are several reasons. **First, Amazon has reach that your other channels do not.** No matter how good your existing sales channels are, there are ideal customers out there who don't know about your products and that your sales teams don't know about. Amazon has over three hundred million US customers in every nook of America and delivers to them in two days or less. Your existing selling channels likely cannot compete with that. As a result, Amazon connects you to new customers that your existing channels miss.

Many of these may be smaller than your typical customers. But Amazon's scale seamlessly rolls up their demand to a much larger market pie. The result is the greatest potential sales market for your products.

Second, Amazon connects you to new markets. Dan typically sells his products to other manufacturers. Traditionally, they buy Dan's products from distributors and industrial supply houses. Each year more of them use Amazon to buy their manufacturing supplies, but that is not Dan's biggest immediate opportunity on Amazon.

To learn that, all he needed to do is check out the reviews on his competitors' bestselling products. He would see that their industrial electronics are a hit among well-moneyed woodworkers and people who like to repair their classic cars. These people want premium products for their weekend hobbies. And they're willing to pay top dollar. Individually, these buyers are too small—Dan's organization and traditional sales channels would never be able to profitably sell to this market. But in aggregate, these hobbyists amount to a multimillion-dollar market, and Dan is missing out on this completely.

Hidden, untapped markets are everywhere. We work with an automotive supply manufacturer that sells into automotive distribution, to auto repair shops, and to auto supply retail. They have hundreds of SKUs that address needs across a variety of automotive categories—solutions for engine maintenance, aftermarket upgrades, cleaning, repairing, and so on.

They've been selling their automotive products on Amazon for several years. And their bestselling automotive SKU is an oil tray . . . that is sold on Amazon as a college dorm room refrigerator liner. They also sell an oil funnel that is quite popular as a beer funnel. Both are large markets they never interacted with through their traditional channels.

If it wasn't for Amazon, we'd never have identified that a large plastic automotive oil tray is the exact size to make sure your dorm fridge doesn't leak on your floor. My client would be selling in the automotive market only. That product is now a bestseller for automotive as well as a bestselling back-to-school item. As a result, he has a more diversified and stronger business for that SKU.

This is not the result you will get for every product you sell. Not every product in your portfolio is destined to be a bestseller or to have exciting new and untapped markets you never considered. But some of them likely will. And until you have your products on Amazon and focus on growing their potential, you have no idea of your catalog's full possibilities.

Third, Amazon's competitive landscape is likely very different. Your top competitors in your traditional channels may not be your top competitors on Amazon. This changes the market dynamics and causes some products to become more or less competitive. Different competition drives different bestsellers.

We will keep saying this—Amazon is a unique market—because it is such an important concept. You can expect to reach new customers that you could not otherwise. Customers will use your products in ways you may not expect. And on Amazon, different competition results in different relative competitive advantages.

Amazon expands your customer base and opens your products to new markets. The full potential of this can only be achieved by focusing on the Amazon channel and setting up your product portfolio to win.

Falsehood #3: "Amazon Is Basically Just Another Customer."

Manufacturers mistakenly think of Amazon as just another customer. Dan expressed this when he commented that Amazon was more difficult than his other customers. He is correct in a sense—the work needed to be successful on Amazon is likely more than a typical retailer.

It's true—Amazon has more requirements and demands than the typical retailer or customer.

However, this is only half the story. Although Amazon is a retailer, they are unique in terms of size, scale, ambition, and opportunity to your business. So you're not doing your business justice by benchmarking the cost to service and level of effort to get Amazon sales against more established, traditional, and slower-growing customers.

Instead, I suggest thinking of Amazon as a distinct channel rather than as just a customer or retailer or e-commerce channel. This is true because not only is their market distinct (see falsehood #1) but also Amazon has unique operational requirements. Between the differences in market, customer, and operations, you're better off thinking of it as its own unique sales channel (with its own unique needs, costs, and potential) rather than as just another customer.

We'll go into more detail on how to meet Amazon's operational requirements in chapter 6, but it's important to understand why Amazon has unique requirements. In short, no other potential customer operates at Amazon's scale.

To quickly put Amazon's scale into perspective, they have more than twelve hundred distribution centers in the US as of this writing. These twelve hundred distribution centers are twice the number that Walmart and UPS have—combined.

Because Amazon operates at a scale unique from all other companies, the requirements to work with them are also unique compared to all other companies. Amazon has demanding operational and cost requirements. These are not designed because Amazon is difficult but because it helps Amazon deliver products to end users more efficiently.

Understanding their mission and aligning to it where it makes sense increases your access to their huge and fast-growing markets and makes you a more efficient company with better operations and better cost structures.

Another reason to consider Amazon as a distinct channel rather than as just another customer is the potential to get higher profits from Amazon compared to other customers. If you are used to wholesale margins, you may be in for a pleasant (and profitable) surprise. The full details are in chapter 5, so this is just a sneak peek. But Amazon has unique margin requirements and opportunities that make it very different from any other channel.

Manufacturers that don't fully appreciate that Amazon is different from other customers and channels will miss Amazon's full potential. They will complain about Amazon's requirements and the cost to serve the account. That Amazon is inflexible. But if you want to succeed, it is critical to recognize what makes Amazon unique and to use that to your business's advantage. Doing this will enable you to evaluate Amazon's true ROI based on the effort and the reward.

Amazon is different from your other customers, and that is a good thing!

Falsehood #4: "I Have Time to Figure This Out."

Back in 1922, my great-grandfather started a feed and grain business in a small Pennsylvania town called Jermyn. In those days, every town needed a flour mill because every town had a bakery where the bread for the town was made. His son took it over and, as you can imagine, times changed. Bread wasn't baked at the corner bakery as much, so his son, my grandfather, transitioned from selling grain and flour to home heating oil and gasoline.

The business was located on the town's main street, so it became immediately successful when he added gas pumps to the front. And because it was a small town where everyone knew one another, he knew who was credit worthy and to whom he could offer fuel oil on house accounts. That new business did really well during the economic boom post–World War II and provided a nice living for his family.

My father joined the company in 1977 with the goal of taking over the business from my grandfather. He learned every aspect, from how to buy fuel oil a few cents cheaper from the Philadelphia depot two hours away to which families never paid their house account on time. The business was successful under my grandfather for over thirty years. My dad figured that as long as he could operate it as well as his father, he would have the same success and prosperity.

He was right . . . for a while. But two external trends were emerging that destroyed that dream.

The first was the hollowing out of small towns. In my grandfather's business, Jermyn was a vibrant semiclosed ecosystem. A town where people lived and knew everyone, where many worked in the town, and where everyone shopped locally. Everyone banked at the Jermyn bank, bought groceries at the Jermyn grocer, and purchased gasoline from my grandfather. By the time my father got involved, that town was dying. And by the mid 1980s, the main street was no longer a destination, with the bank and grocer closed.

The second trend was a technology innovation—the rise of credit cards and pay-at-the-pump options. My father's customers paid primarily in cash or house credit. My father, like many merchants at the time, didn't like credit cards due to the fees and overhead. My father already had the house credit program, so in his mind, credit cards were unnecessary. He reluctantly added a credit card machine only after customers insisted. But it wasn't at the pump, and cash was always encouraged.

The problem was that by not really embracing the trend, he encouraged his customers who were warming up to credit cards to look elsewhere. And he gave his competitors who were more credit card friendly and who had installed pay-at-the-pump readers a small opening. Over time, as the trend continued, he started to lose customers to the competition.

By the time he decided to fully embrace the credit card trend, it was too late. Too many customers had already changed their behavior and were in the habit of shopping elsewhere. My father's business never recovered and eventually closed.

Dan understood this about Amazon. He didn't like Amazon, didn't understand who was buying on Amazon, and didn't know how to work with Amazon, but he did know that he couldn't ignore Amazon and had to do something about it now. That's why he gave me a call.

Although Amazon has been around for more than three decades, its impact on any given market today, so far, can vary considerably. Each market on Amazon is a bit different.

There are markets such as consumer electronics that are extremely mature and hypercompetitive. Every company already has an Amazon presence. If there are any remaining holdouts, they're likely too late to economically become competitive on Amazon. It would just cost too much to build the traffic and sales from scratch against extremely well-entrenched competitors.

On the other hand, there are markets on Amazon with no major competitors or significant sales today, so far. This is becoming less and less common, but you can still find specialized niche categories where there are few to no products. There are many niches in the industrial space or B2B space where only a few products exist on Amazon. These greenfield niches are rare but allow a forward-thinking manufacturer to own the market and develop it as it grows.

And there are still thousands of categories where there isn't a dominant brand with a strong right to win. I'd go so far as to say that most categories still have an opportunity where a manufacturer with quality products can get a reasonable immediate return on their investment and stake a claim on a growing market.

But as more and more manufacturers in a particular market niche realize this opportunity, they make it increasingly more difficult for the next entrant to reproduce their success. The market is large and growing, but there will be only a finite number of winners. That eventually leads to a point where it is no longer immediately profitable for new entrants to succeed.

That is why it's critical to have a plan *now*.

The next couple of chapters arm you with the information you'll need to formulate the perfect plan for your company. Before we dive into that, it's a good idea to get a baseline on where your company, industry, and markets are relative to Amazon.

This is a useful exercise whether you already sell to Amazon or whether you have never sold your product there.

Go on Amazon right now. We'll start by doing branded searches—searches that include your brand name(s). If your company is XYZ Corp and you sell Acme-branded driveway sealers, a good starting point would be the following: "XYZ Corp" and "XYZ driveway sealer" and "Acme driveway sealer."

These branded searches are the type that your existing and most loyal customers conduct. What do these customers see? Even if you do not sell on Amazon, resellers may be buying your products from you and reselling on Amazon. Are they doing your products justice?

Then do some branded searches for your top competitors. How are they doing?

Finally, do some generic searches. These are unbranded searches that refer to the product category, product function, or solution ("driveway sealer" or "blacktop sealer" in this example). How do your products and your competitors' products rank in the search results? Products at the top of the page get the vast majority of the sales. Are your products there?

Get a sense for the state of *your* Amazon market today:

- Did the searches return what you expected?
- Was it easy to find your products?
- Are your products even being sold? Your competitions' products?

Click on the top listings:

- How do the listings compare across brands?
- Based on what you see, whose products would you buy?
- Who has the most reviews?
- Who appears to be winning?

Scroll through the search results and make note of who is advertising. (Advertised listings will have a small SPONSORED label next to them.) Advertising is a growth strategy, and brands that advertise generally do better than brands that don't.

Read some reviews and see what people like and dislike about the top products. Any unexpected uses? How do your products compare?

Then think about your business and its relationship with Amazon. Do you sell to Amazon? Are you making the mistake of treating Amazon as just another customer? The products you see at the top of the searches you conducted are winning on Amazon today because they are focusing on Amazon as a channel. Are you actively managing and developing Amazon to be successful?

Finally, no matter what you find today, ask yourself where you think the Amazon market will be in five years. It will likely grow 10 to 20 percent year over year of compounding growth. The top brands in that category can capture a majority of the sales. Picture how large the market will become and what it means to your company to have a sales leadership role in that category.

Dan recognized that potential in Amazon and summed up his current situation: "Clearly we are not doing this right. Everyone else is doing really well, but we are struggling. I think Amazon is a necessary evil. And we need help now to figure it out." Dan understood that he must reengage now with Amazon.

That's where this book's guidance comes in. The next several chapters will lay out exactly what it takes to win on Amazon. But before we talk about how to make *you* successful on Amazon, we first need to understand what makes Amazon so successful. My late business partner worked at Amazon for many years and onboarded one of Dan's competitors. We'll share that story in the next chapter.

CHAPTER 3

HOW AMAZON CAN SELL YOUR PRODUCTS BETTER THAN YOU CAN

Bill Grdanski grew up in a small steel town in Pittsburgh. As a kid, he helped his dad fix cars. That led him to study mechanical engineering after high school, where he ultimately got a job servicing turbine engines. Bill liked to work with his hands, he liked manufacturing, and he considered himself blue collar even after he quickly rose to more managerial roles. He excelled at operational consulting in the paper industry and in other commodity industries.

When he told me he joined Amazon back in 2009, I was a bit surprised at first. Amazon was a dot-com tech company, and it wasn't immediately clear why a blue-collar kid from Pittsburgh would have any interest in them. Or why high-tech Amazon would have any interest in Bill. After all, he was the guy I knew who had a ten-year-old laptop and typed with two fingers.

It seemed like such a bad fit from both sides.

But I couldn't have been more wrong. I completely mischaracterized Amazon as a company. I didn't understand what they did and why it was different. I just thought they were another tech company and another retailer. And because of this, I missed what attracted Bill to them and why Bill and Amazon were such a good fit.

I have grown to view Amazon as an engine that is designed to deliver products that people want.

The engine metaphor is very deliberate. Engines are physical, mechanical systems. Although Amazon is best known for its website and is a high-tech company, what makes it unique and special among the world's largest corporations is their real-world operations. Their operations start with the manufacturers and stop when the end user receives the product. Engines are complex systems that operate with certain speeds and efficiency. Amazon is hyperfocused on improvement and tries to operate that engine faster and faster with more and more efficiency.

Understanding Amazon's focus removes a lot of the mystery. If you can understand why they operate as they do, you can use that knowledge to develop a plan to win.

For example, because Amazon is just an engine to deliver products to people, they don't care what products they deliver. It can be your products or your competitors' products. Amazon wins as long as they deliver more and more.

For you to win on Amazon, you must understand Amazon's motivations in detail and make a deliberate plan that aligns with their goals. The better you align with Amazon's goals, the more of your products Amazon will sell and deliver. The Amazon engine is growing in size and speed every year, and companies that understand it benefit from the growth it drives.

Amazon's Flywheel: The Secret to Amazon's Growth

Amazon uses a similar analogy to describe what makes them unique. The following chart is called the Amazon flywheel, and it was drawn on a napkin back in 2001 by Jeff Bezos to describe how Amazon operates and drives growth:[1]

---

[1] Amazon.com, "About Amazon," accessed September 22, 2023, www.amazon.jobs/en/landing_pages/about-amazon.

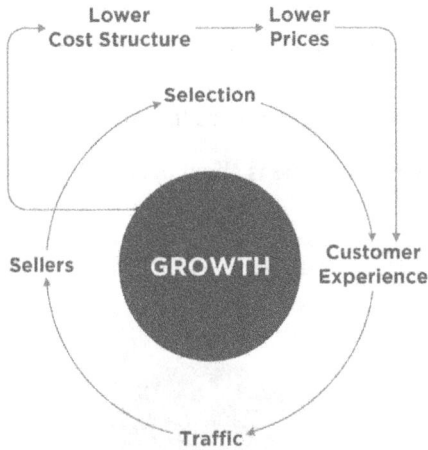

The graphic contains two self-reinforcing closed loops (or virtuous cycles) designed to drive growth.

The first virtuous cycle is about the customers:

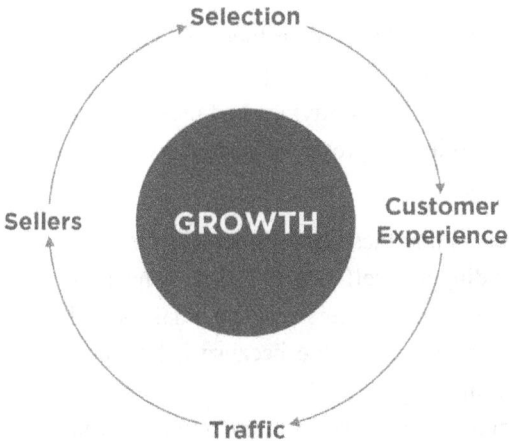

1. Good customer experience drives more customer visits and more traffic.

2. More traffic attracts more sellers and manufacturers to the platform.

3. More sellers and manufacturers increase the selection available to buy.

4. Increased selection improves the customer experience.

The second virtuous cycle is about operations and costs:

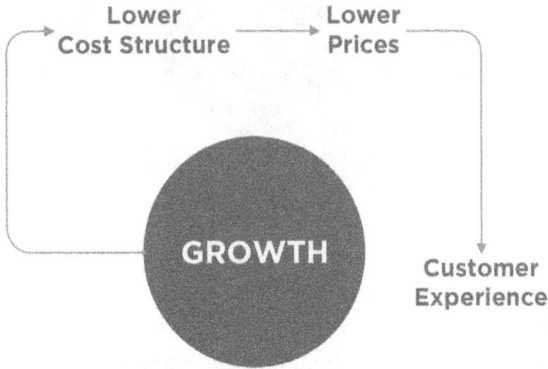

```
        Lower              Lower
   ──►  Cost Structure ──► Prices ──┐
  ┌─►                                │
  │                                  │
  │          ╭─────────╮             ▼
  │          │ GROWTH  │        Customer
  └──────────╰─────────╯        Experience
```

1. Amazon's scale and their focus on operations create a lower cost structure.

2. Amazon takes that savings and uses it to lower prices.

3. Lower prices improve the customer experience and contribute to the first loop.

The magic is that these closed loops or virtuous cycles drive growth in a compounding and self-fulfilling way. Amazon is the most attractive marketplace for manufacturers because it has the traffic, and it's the most trafficked e-commerce website because it has the most manufacturers. Growth drives more growth.

The virtuous cycle drives momentum in Amazon's business and results in winner-takes-all successes. Amazon knew this early on and explicitly looks for virtuous cycles in all aspects of their business.

Their quest to constantly improve shipping speed is another example of a virtuous cycle. Customers go to Amazon because they have fast delivery. The increased volume enables Amazon to deliver at a lower cost, which allows them to invest more in delivery speed.

Kindle is yet another virtuous cycle. Kindle gives customers a library and an instant bookstore in their pocket. It provides great customer experience, which causes shoppers to buy more books through Kindle, which makes the platform more desirable for publishers, which makes Kindle more compelling for customers.

Amazon's Flywheel Can Drive Your Success

The key to the virtuous cycle is that success drives success. And the magical part is that as a manufacturer, you can participate in the cycle and benefit from the growth it creates.

Here is how a savvy manufacturer fits into the Amazon flywheel. Let's take a look at the first virtuous cycle:

- *Customer experience:* Amazon gives you tools to market your product pages and make them your virtual salesperson. By educating Amazon customers on your products, you give them a good experience with your brand and help them make better buying decisions.
- *Traffic:* Amazon rewards products that sell with traffic that drives more sales. This is its own virtuous cycle, and we refer to it as momentum. Creating momentum is a key concept that we teach in chapter XX and is essential to creating bestsellers and long-term sales growth.
- *Sales:* More traffic leads to more sales, which makes Amazon a more significant channel in your business.
- *Selection:* Sales incentivize you to add more of your catalog. We advocate for adding your entire catalog as quickly as possible. Amazon has infinite shelf space, and there are customers out there for each and every one of your products. As our clients have greater and greater success on Amazon, most start developing Amazon-only products to further expand their selection.

And larger selection brings us back to a better customer experience! A key implication is that Amazon's flywheel grows the size of your market over time on their site. Turning a small (or nonexistent) market into a large market improves the customer experience, and making a large market even larger improves customer experience even more. The flywheel ensures long term-market growth.

Another implication concerns momentum in the virtuous cycle. Because traffic drives sales, which brings more traffic, products that win continue to win. Once you start getting sales momentum, it has a tendency to grow on its own. The virtuous cycle makes Amazon a winner-takes-most market.

Bestsellers can be created on Amazon. And once you are a bestseller, you get most of the traffic. That naturally makes it difficult for competitors to unseat you. They need to work very hard to steal that traffic away, but you do not have to work nearly as hard to defend your bestselling position.

Generating and maintaining sales momentum is critical to developing a long-term successful Amazon business. The best part is that you're creating sales momentum on a winner-takes-most market that is rapidly growing. Therefore, the earlier you enter, invest to win, and execute properly, the bigger and more enduring the payoff. Luckily, you are reading this book, which will teach you exactly how to do that.

But that's not all. Your story is not complete until you understand the impact of the second virtuous cycle on your business. As we discussed, the second virtuous cycle is that Amazon is creating lower cost structures and increased operational efficiencies for the customer's benefit.

There are several implications related to Amazon's focus on cost savings.

First, Amazon is willing to sell and distribute your products for below-industry margins. Any cost savings they can generate, they will pass on to the consumer. Given that Amazon is willing to operate on slim margins, you potentially have better margins with Amazon than with other retailers or customers. If you are pricing Amazon like other customers, you are doing it wrong. This concept is so important that we devote all of chapter 5 to maximizing your margin with Amazon.

Second, Amazon is hyperfocused on operational efficiency. They have a variety of industry-leading programs to make receiving products more efficient. This includes packaging innovations, product and carton labeling, and a variety of shipping methods. There is a good chance that your company can't meet all their requirements today. Upgrading your capabilities not only takes costs out of working with Amazon but also makes you more efficient with your other customers. In fact, we've heard from clients that other major e-retailers are beginning to adopt similar operational requirements as Amazon. Developing e-commerce-grade operations will help future-proof your organization.

Third, Amazon's flywheel has implications for product development. Certain products are more efficient for Amazon to sell. The more efficient your products are, the more they align to Amazon's virtuous cycle (and the more you'll sell!). By making subtle changes to products you already have, you can massively increase the value proposition to Amazon and their customers and to your bottom line.

Taking a step back, the Amazon flywheel illustrates the long-term perspective that Amazon has with regard to their (and your) markets. Amazon is extremely patient. They are willing to experiment and invest for a very long time with the expectation that the payoff may take several years to materialize. This long-term thinking is extremely powerful, as it permits them to build out systems that support tremendous scale and unparalleled cost structures well beyond what the market demands today.

For markets where Amazon has less penetration, this long-term perspective represents tremendous opportunity for the current participants. No matter how large or small the market is today—whether it is so small that it's insignificant, acceptable to ignore, or large—it can grow quickly. The Amazon flywheel ensures that when the right customers and products come to them, there is a massive system under it that can ramp up to much larger future demand.

This is why Amazon can be such a risk to companies that ignore it. The iceberg may appear to be small, but if you don't share their long-term perspective, you may learn exactly how large and devastating the iceberg can be.

Now freeze that thought. For a moment, try to ignore everything I've shared with you. In fact, forget about Amazon's focus on customer experience and that year after year Amazon is relentlessly working toward making them your end user's shopping choice. And I want you to forget the years of investment in building a marketplace that becomes faster and more efficient over time and as they grow.

Instead, I want you to ask yourself: *What is an ideal customer?*

Go ahead.

Got it?

OK. Good.

I'm sure you'd say that they're great to work with and buy a ton of products. Amazon can also be great to work with—as long as you understand what to expect. But let's quantify exactly what a top customer would look like for you. How much of your catalog would they buy? What would the sales be? What kind of growth do you want? Be realistic.

I want you to get this picture in your head because, in the next chapter, we're going to see whether Amazon can be an ideal customer for you.

But first, let's meet back up with Bill.

Bill went on to have a very successful career at Amazon. One of his roles was onboarding manufacturers and making them successful. His first challenge was addressing manufacturers' common misconceptions (see chapter 2). But the most important part of his pitch was when he shared the Amazon flywheel.

The reason was simple. Bill onboarded more than one hundred manufacturers in under two years, from Fortune 50 companies to mom-and-pop specialty manufacturers. What he found was that companies that understood how Amazon operates performed better on Amazon than those that didn't.

Not every company he worked with was successful. Some had an adversarial relationship with Amazon almost immediately. Every Amazon requirement was met with pushback—"We don't do it that way." They failed to see that Amazon is intentionally designed to support its flywheel and that the goal is to create the largest potential marketplace. But if a company failed to see that or could not adapt, it never worked out well.

Many of the companies Bill onboarded, however, did understand and were able to carve out a successful market and to benefit from the Amazon flywheel. In the next chapter, I will show you how to estimate exactly how big your market is on Amazon, today and in the future.

CHAPTER 4

HOW BIG THE AMAZON PIE IS
FOR YOUR BUSINESS (AND WHY IT
KEEPS GETTING BIGGER)

Jerome's company had been selling on Amazon for several years. "It's pretty much been on autopilot," he said. "Amazon helped us get started a couple of years back and then we filled their orders."

Already I suspected Jerome's company as leaving a ton of money on the table. Although Amazon can be relatively easy to work with, it's not a set-and-forget type of business. Without ongoing maintenance and monitoring, sales start to slow and opportunities get missed.

Jerome continued. "Amazon is growing really well. Right now it's our biggest online channel and has been growing at over seven percent year over year. We expect to do three million dollars this year." He seemed very satisfied with that performance.

My initial suspicion was confirmed. Although I didn't yet know much about Jerome's company's market on Amazon, I do know that a well-managed product portfolio should be growing faster than that.

After all, Amazon has been growing around 10+ percent. Although every category is a bit different, I would expect Jerome's to grow much faster than average. And a well-managed portfolio can grow much more than the category. So if Amazon is growing faster than his Amazon business and his category is growing faster than Amazon, then his company's market share is actually shrinking!

Jerome called because they were starting a strategic planning process for the next year and wanted us to do a market analysis. They wanted to understand the total market size and whether there would be a significant additional return in focusing on Amazon. Jerome's sense was that they were doing very well (in his mind), but he wondered if they could double sales in the next couple of years.

We agreed to help him find out.

In this chapter, I'm going to share exactly what we did to calculate Jerome's market opportunity on Amazon. He paid us $10,000 to do the analysis and provide him with strategic recommendations. After reading this book, you'll be able to complete the same analysis on your own business for free.

This chapter will even cover a shortcut method we use to quickly estimate market size when you just need a ballpark answer.

Jerome thought his $3 million in sales was pretty good. But without understanding the full size of his addressable market, he really didn't know. Jerome had a good sense of where his company ranked in the overall market versus his competitors. But he had no idea how his company ranked in the Amazon space.

If the entire addressable market was $10 million and he captured 30 percent, then maybe that is strong performance. But what if the addressable market was $100 million? Was 3 percent of the market all that Jerome's company deserved to win?

The truth is, you don't know until you look. And in my experience, when you look, the size of the Amazon market is probably larger than you think.

For example, if I asked you how many air filters amazon sold in the US, what would your guess be? How about screws? Cat leashes?

Consider these numbers in the year this book was published:

- Amazon will have sold approximately $800 million worth of air filters in 2023. This includes both residential and industrial air filters, with the vast majority of sales in the residential market. This excludes air filtering systems.

- Amazon will have sold approximately $50 million in screws in 2023. Wood screws are the most popular category, followed by concrete and drywall.
- Amazon will have sold over $20 million in cat leashes in 2023. This includes both leashes and harnesses to walk your cat but excludes any dual use dog leashes.

How close were your guesses? I spend hours every day on Amazon and manage multiple millions of spend a month, and I am still surprised by their market sizes. When you sell more than $500 billion in products a year, even the smallest niche can be huge.

Let's go through the process of determining how big your market is on Amazon.

Defining Your Market

The first step is defining exactly what your market is on Amazon. In general, the size of your market is the total value of your sales and all your competitors' similar product sales.

This is true for Amazon, but there is a twist in how you define your competition. Competition on Amazon is measured by searches. So if you sell chewing gum, your chewing gum competitors are not only the top competitors you know from being in the business for years but also every relevant competitor that shows up when a consumer searches for "chewing gum" on Amazon.

The reason you define your competition according to searches rather than similar products is because that is how Amazon customers operate. When they want to buy gum, they search for "gum," "chewing gum," or "bubble gum" and get access to the entire market. (Search terms are the phrases customers use to look for a particular product.) You want to view it in the same way as a potential buyer when analyzing your market. You might find some competitors or products that weren't on your radar.

For example, if a manufacturer only focuses on the national leading brands of gum and gum they see in store shelves, they are missing an important emerging segment. eCommerce dominant brands may be small today but are growing rapidly. In the case of bubble gum, at least

30 percent of the Amazon market are competitors that are not on the top national brand list.

Here are the top brands on Amazon as of August 2023:

Top Amazon Brands

1	Mentos
2	Trident
3	Ice Breakers
4	**PUR**
5	Extra
6	Orbit
7	**Epic**
8	Eclipse Gum
9	Dentyne
10	Juicy Fruit Gum
11	5 Gum
12	**Big League Chew**
13	**Jawliner**
14	**Falim**
15	**Simply Gum**
16	**Tootsie Roll**
17	Doublemint
18	Bubble Yum
19	**Freedent**
20	Wrigley's

Each of these is a multimillion-dollar brand on Amazon. The brands highlighted in boldface are top sellers on Amazon but are not on the top national brand list. In a few years, there is a good chance they will be.

Additionally, notice that several of the top national brands (like Chiclets and Stride) are not bestsellers on Amazon. They have strong national brand recognition but are being beaten by more Amazon-savvy brands. Amazon is a new frontier with very different competitors from your other channels.

This simple example illustrates that the way to identify your market on Amazon is through completing searches like an end user. Each search returns a list of the most relevant products for that search, with the top-selling and most advertised products for that search appearing toward the top.

So your market is the sum of all relevant products returned by the complete set of search terms customers use to find products in your market. It sounds a bit circular, but I promise it is not!

In other words, the search terms people use to search for products like yours define the market. The market size is how much relevant product Amazon sells from those searches.

Although there are technically an infinite number of search terms, it turns out that they cluster and return similar results. While there is only some product overlap between "bubble gum" and "chewing gum," there is a great deal of overlap between "sugar free gum" and "gum sugar free." So you don't need to identify every possible way a user would search for your products to get competitive results. Only the most popular and distinct searches are necessary. A handful of search terms will often drive the vast majority of sales for a given product.

But what if you don't know how people search for your products? There are tools out there that can take a product and let you know what people search for when they buy it. We have internal tools that provide these insights, but there are third-party data providers like Helium 10, which has a decent free plan, that offer this type of data as well.

Whether you start with products or obvious words that people use to search for your products, you should end up with a list of search terms.

When we're hired by a client to do a full market analysis, this is the exact approach we take. We start with their products and their competitors' products, identify key search terms for those products, see what products it returns, and repeat. Depending on the scope, we'll do this many times over. When we did this for Jerome, we identified approximately twenty key search terms that returned almost two thousand unique products.

The challenge here is that not all two thousand products have significant sales or are even part of the addressable market. If you are a sugar-free gum manufacturer, you might not care how big the sugared gum market is. Additionally, some of the estimated two thousand product sales were so small that they were insignificant.

Estimating Product Sales

The next step is to estimate the product sales. Amazon publishes a sales metric for most products called Best Sellers Rank. As of this writing, the twelve pack of "The Official Big League Chew Original Bubble Gum" has a Best Sellers Rank of #873 in the grocery and gourmet food category and #22 in the chewing gum category:

Product details

Is Discontinued By Manufacturer : No

Package Dimensions : 11.14 x 5.87 x 2.64 inches; 1.76 Pounds

UPC : 042897959078 042897959191

Manufacturer : Ford Gum Inc.

ASIN : B00BPXN1OC

Best Sellers Rank: #873 in Grocery & Gourmet Food (See Top 100 in Grocery & Gourmet Food)
  #22 in Chewing Gum

This means that the Big League Chewing Gum page is the twenty-second most popular product by sales volume in the chewing gum category. And it's the 873rd most popular item sold by sales volume in the grocery and gourmet food category.

Amazon categorizes every product it sells and provides a sales ranking for most. The twenty-second most popular product in a category sells more units than the twenty-third and fewer units than the twenty-first. And if you know the sales of the twenty-first and the twenty-third most popular products, you can easily estimate the sales of Big League Chewing Gum.

Companies with access to large catalogs of products have used this same logic to generate algorithms that do exactly that. You give them a Best Sellers Rank, and they provide the current daily or monthly sales volume. (Helium 10 and Jungle Scout are two that offer this as a free service.)

Although this is just an estimate, it's pretty good in most cases. We use these tools daily and often sanity check their estimated sales against actual sales data. Estimates are usually within 20 percent, and when they are used across multiple products, the errors seem to cancel out.

Determining Your Market Size

You have identified the key search terms that define your market. You found all the relevant products. Now you just have to generate sales estimates using the Amazon Best Sellers Rank and roll it up to get the market size.

Here's the process as a graphic:

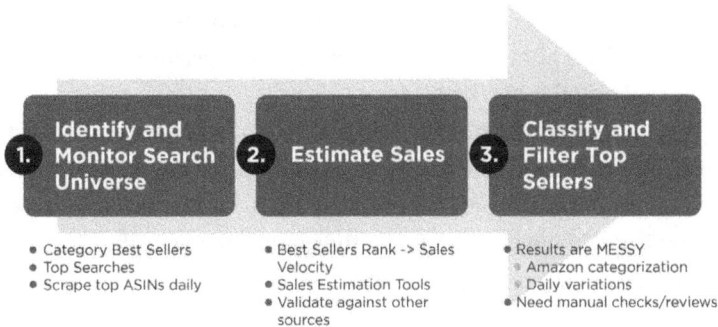

1. Identify and Monitor Search Universe	2. Estimate Sales	3. Classify and Filter Top Sellers
• Category Best Sellers • Top Searches • Scrape top ASINs daily	• Best Sellers Rank -> Sales Velocity • Sales Estimation Tools • Validate against other sources	• Results are MESSY • Amazon categorization • Daily variations • Need manual checks/reviews

Depending on the number of products in your market, this can be a fairly large undertaking. For example, the two thousand products we identified earlier in the chapter break down as follows:

```
┌─────────────────────┐                    ┌─────────────────────┐
│   Initial Universe  │                    │      In Scope       │
│     2000 ASINs      │────────────────────│     300 ASINs       │
│   Prelim. Estimate  │                    │      $70M/yr        │
│   $300-$600M/yr     │                    └─────────────────────┘
└─────────────────────┘
                                           ┌─────────────────────┐
                                           │    Out of Scope     │
                        ───────────────────│     600 ASINs       │
                                           │   $200 - $400M/yr   │
                                           └─────────────────────┘

                                           ┌─────────────────────┐
                                           │        TBD          │
                        ───────────────────│     1100 ASINs      │
                                           │    $40-$60M/yr      │
                                           └─────────────────────┘
```

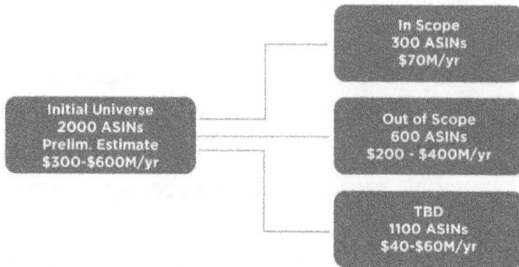

We identified two thousand products in key search results from our selected search terms. We categorized the top nine hundred products and found that three hundred were part of the addressable market. Six hundred were in adjacent (related but out of scope) markets. Eleven hundred products had sales that were insignificant to the analysis.

Out of the $70 million addressable market, the client had 4 percent market penetration on Amazon (versus approximately 20+ percent in the market overall). The client was significantly underperforming on Amazon relative to their other markets.

This not only let the client know how much they were underperforming on Amazon but also opened the client's eyes to a key adjacent market. They had products and services on their shelf for one of those adjacent markets. But without the insights of the market analysis, they never considered Amazon as a viable channel.

Quick and Dirty Market Analysis Option

Admittedly, this can be a lot to pull together on your own. We provide various levels of market analysis and monitoring as a service for companies that do not want to go through this manual work. But not everyone needs this level of detail.

In many cases, you can take a shortcut and use Amazon's bestseller pages (see www.amazon.co/Best-Sellers/zgbs) to find the categories most relevant to your products.

The bestseller pages show the top-selling products by velocity. The number one spot is the product in that category that has sold the most units. For example, you can see the top chewing gums on Amazon here: www.amazon.com/gp/bestsellers/grocery/16322471/ref=pd_zg_hrsr_grocery.

If you sign up for Helium 10's free browser plug-in, you can use it to estimate the monthly sales for the top fifty chewing gum products. At the time of this writing, it amounts to $6.2 million a month at retail. By going to the next page, you can see that the top fifty-one to one hundred products amount to $2.6 million a month. This works out that the top fifty drive 70 percent of the top one hundred sales.

If the top fifty-one to one hundred is just a small fraction of the top fifty, you can use the estimated sales for these two pages to approximate the size of the market overall. In this situation, we assume that the top one hundred products represent 80 percent of the overall market.

If the top fifty-one to one hundred is 25 percent or more of the top one hundred, then the market is very large, and the top one hundred likely represent a smaller fraction of the overall opportunity. Even in these situations, the estimated sales of the top one hundred products give you a good indication of the overall market size. Without doing the full analysis here, given that the top fifty-one to one hundred is around 30 percent of the top one hundred, we would assume that the entire category is about $12 to $14 million per month at retail.

Can't Find Your Market on Amazon?

This happens less often these days, but occasionally we talk to companies that do not have established markets on Amazon.

We did this analysis for a company that is a leader in their industry with over $2 billion in revenue per year. They sell mostly B2B and wanted to know their Amazon opportunity.

They had multiple product categories, each with significant sales through traditional channels. They were distinct enough that each product category was a separate market analysis.

Most of their product categories had multimillion-dollar opportunities. They were decent-size markets, without a clear market leader, and appearing to grow fast. Ideal opportunities for a determined and well-funded market leader.

But two product categories had nearly no market on Amazon.

In these situations, you need to dig a bit deeper. Some product categories are so poorly represented that there just isn't a market today. Other products just do not sell well on Amazon. Determining which type of market you have can be tricky.

If you find that your market has limited product selection and that the product pages do a poor job of selling the products, you may have a case where the market is just underdeveloped. If customers can't find the products they want to buy, then the market will have no sales.

One of the client's product categories fell into this situation. We could see customers searching for products, and logically it made sense that there would be demand for the category. But the market size did not show evidence of sales. The reason was that none of the major competitors focused on listing their products on Amazon, so customers didn't have serious options to buy.

When we listed our customer's products, sales came almost immediately! Selection created customer demand, just as the Amazon flywheel predicted.

The other special case when you see a market with limited sales is that it's just a bad market on Amazon. I believe that this situation is more rare than you think and that you can sell almost anything on Amazon, but even I admit there are certain limitations.

When a market has limited sales, it's usually driven by special characteristics of the customer, not the product. You can sell highly specialized or technical products on Amazon. But you can't really sell if the customer isn't coming to Amazon to find it.

In the case of our client, the product was a specialized tool that is sold along with other services. The market is large overall, but all the customers and potential customers have established relationships with traditional suppliers due to the services involved. Logically, it made sense that the Amazon market would be small, and we could confirm it, as another competitor listed their selection and did a decent job of marketing their products. The market had sufficient selection but no customers.

Actual Market Potential: Potentially Big, Definitely Growing

Here is a formula for market potential:

Your Sales Potential = Size of Market × Your Rightful Share × Market Growth

At the end of the day, it's not just how big the market is today but how big the market will be and how much you can capture.

You can win in several different ways:

- Get a small slice of a fast-growing market.
- Get a large slice of a small market.
- Get a small slice of a huge market.
- Get a small slice that grows.

Amazon retail grows at 10+ percent a year, with most of the growth coming from buyers purchasing more and more from Amazon over time. They are gaining a greater share of most markets every year.

Without knowing anything more about your particular market, you can expect a random market to grow the same amount as Amazon overall. More than 10 percent year-over-year growth is great growth.

Additionally, markets have the potential to grow many times Amazon's average. This is true for markets that are just starting out on the Amazon flywheel—markets with limited product representation or markets where customers have limited experience switching from traditional channels to Amazon.

If you have a market like this, develop your Amazon presence now to stake a claim once the Amazon flywheel starts taking off. We've seen five to ten times sales growth in markets like that.

More mature markets can have average or slightly less than Amazon's average growth. That's still not a shabby number. Even in markets that you would consider extremely mature—where customers have been going to Amazon for years to buy products and every product is represented, you can expect markets to grow higher than the market's overall average due to the convenience effect. Every year, customers buy more and more online.

The second aspect of growth is how much share you can take in a market.

It's your right to win. If you have great products or great pricing, you should expect to be able to take a significant share. Because Amazon is a winner-takes-most market, products and brands with a competitive advantage do extra well on their platform.

But Amazon also awards execution. That's why a no-name brand running out of someone's garage can beat an industry-leading manufacturer. The start-up didn't make better products; they just knew how to execute better on Amazon.

Your rightful share on Amazon is your right to win combined with your ability to execute. The magic foundation to win on Amazon is great products at a great price with flawless execution.

You build that foundation and let the Amazon flywheel take care of the rest. You can expect a dominant position in the market today and that the market will be among your fastest growing.

To get started, you need to do two things:

1. *Determine your market size.* Understand its size and growth potential.
2. *Confirm your right to win.* Do your brand, products, and pricing offer exceptional value in that market?

If you have a market that is either large or has the potential to be large and has a clear right to win, then you have the ingredients to win on Amazon.

The remainder of this book will walk you through how to turn your winning products and the Amazon opportunity into a strong and successful business. We cover the exact steps we use ourselves to develop bestselling products and category market leaders. Winning on Amazon is simply a process or a recipe—now that you have the right ingredients, you just need to take the right steps and success will come.

It sure did for Jerome. He was selling $3 million but suspected that his company could be making much more and shared that his goal was to double the business in the next couple of years. We followed the same process as outlined in this chapter and found the addressable market to be $70 million and growing at about the same as Amazon overall. He had roughly a 5 percent share of the Amazon market, and his share was decreasing each year.

We worked with his team to put together a plan to fix that. He paid a lot of money for that plan, but you'll get the thinking behind it and the same tactics in the next couple of chapters for the price of this book.

His company hired us to execute the plan. For many companies, it's more effective to outsource specialist expertise than to try to bring it in-house. The company goal for us was to double the business in the next couple of years. We didn't do that. Instead, we tripled the business in exactly twenty-four months, taking the Amazon business from $3 million a year to over $9 million.

The next several chapters explain how you can achieve similar success.

CHAPTER 5

HOW TO SET UP YOUR AMAZON ACCOUNT SO THAT YOU WIN IN THE SHORT RUN AND DOMINATE IN THE LONG TERM

A t Mantaro Partners, we can help three types of companies. **The first type are manufacturers with an existing Amazon relationship and that are feeling pain.** These are companies that have problems and are struggling. I say they're in pain because that's how they describe it. It could be that their sales are flat or declining when they know their competitors are growing, that they're not getting paid, that they're getting killed with charge-backs and shortages, or that they're just not working well with Amazon's systems.

These clients know it's not working, but they don't always know why or what to do about it. The first step with a manufacturer that is feeling pain from Amazon is to diagnose the situation, get to the root cause, and provide a workable path out of their pain.

The biggest challenge with these companies is that they likely have multiple issues and may not even know about all of them. It's very much a situation of peeling the onion to uncover everything. A lot of their problems stem from the falsehoods described in chapter 2 or from the pitfalls explained in chapter 10.

Identifying and fixing every issue can take some time. So does unlearning bad habits. But the great thing about working with these clients is that they generally are doing some things right (as evidenced by existing sales), and we can really throw gas on the fire of growth once the problems are solved.

The second type are the Amazon virgins—manufacturers that have never sold to Amazon. There are not as many companies that are new to Amazon as there used to be—every year there are fewer and fewer as more take the Amazon plunge.

Clients that are new to Amazon are great to work with, as there are no historical mistakes that need to be undone.

The biggest challenge is that they don't know what they don't know. These companies must ensure that they have a solid understanding of Amazon before they take the plunge. We covered many of the basics they need to know in chapter 3. But once they are properly educated on the Amazon principles and trained on how Amazon operates, they can be great to work with.

The third type are manufacturers that are selling and that believe everything is going well. They don't have any major problems. At least, none that they're aware of. They're very happy with how things are going. For most, Amazon is a significant account and often one of their fastest growing.

Honestly, these are frequently the hardest to convince that they can benefit from outside help. After all, they're doing great from their perspective. We've had a divisional head brag about their 7 percent growth on Amazon because it beat their company average 3 percent growth. He was happy because the high relative growth got his bonus maxed out.

What he and his company didn't realize was the huge missed opportunity. They didn't see that their product category was growing over 20 percent and that they had a right to win a much larger share.

If you think 7 percent growth is fantastic, imagine what achieving 30 to 40 percent growth would be like. The biggest obstacle companies like that face in achieving those kinds of amazing results is realizing that it's even possible.

A good place for these companies to start is to understand their market opportunity, as outlined in chapter 4. It's also helpful to do a full audit on their account to identify what opportunities they may be missing. It's rare that we encounter an account where there isn't an opportunity to add significant incremental revenue and profit.

The interesting thing is that although each of these types of companies has different initial problems and challenges, the plan to grow their businesses (after solving their initial problems) is largely the same. In this chapter, I cover the strategic framework we use. It's the same framework we implement when we sign a new client.

The framework can take an Amazon newbie and put them on the path to success. It will help a struggling business identify their issues and prioritize what they need to fix. And it helps a successful business locate the best opportunities to pour gas on their growth.

This one-size-fits-all framework is perfect to help create the best growth plan for any company at any phase in their Amazon relationship. We'll go into all of its great details momentarily, but before we do, we need to make sure your company is ready to proceed.

Necessary Prerequisites for Working with Amazon

Amazon is not the easiest company to work with (for reasons we already explained). Over the years, we've developed a short list of minimum requirements that a company should be able to meet before focusing on building an Amazon business.

If you are new to Amazon or if your Amazon business is struggling, you should review these to make sure your company can meet them.

There are just three prerequisites, but without them you cannot win on Amazon. If your organization is not comfortable with these, then it probably makes sense to focus on meeting the requirements before focusing on Amazon.

1. Do you have a right to win on Amazon?

Ideally, your product is superior (faster, cheaper, better) to the competition. But the minimum requirement is that your products are comparable to the competition on Amazon in price and quality.

We cover retail pricing in great detail in chapter 6, but your manufacturing costs should be aggressive to the competition on Amazon for the same quality. It's always good to do a detailed pricing analysis to confirm that you have enough margin to match or beat the current Amazon competition.

For example, a household products manufacturer approached us about adding their products to Amazon. They are manufactured in Vietnam while the leading competitors on Amazon manufacture their products in China. The product was largely a commodity, so there were no major quality differences.

Vietnam had a lower cost of goods than China, so they had a price advantage—that was their right to win.

This's why we love to work with US-based manufacturing companies. Although the manufacturing costs may be higher, the real and perceived quality of a product that is made in the USA is higher too. This is a right to win as well.

Another right to win can be your brand. If your brand is recognizable, people will choose your products over a no-name competitive product at the same price.

A clear reason to buy your products over the existing competition on Amazon is your right to win, and you must have one.

2. Do you have a reliable supply chain?

This might seem like a basic question, but I have seen this impact so many companies. Tariffs, staffing factories, sourcing, pandemics, and inflation have and continue to cause issues.

Succeeding on Amazon does require an investment of time and resources. And that investment pays off only if you have a product to sell. There is nothing more frustrating to finally start seeing success on the Amazon channel only to then stockout of products. The Amazon flywheel requires a steady and growing supply of products for it to work.

We've talked about growing sales momentum. Stocking out of product kills momentum and lets the competition take your sales. In many ways, building momentum after a stockout is like starting from scratch on the product all over again. That's why a reliable supply chain with few to no out-of-stock situations is key.

The requirement here is being able to ship your product catalog reliably and without backorders. That means maintaining a certain level of inventory in the US and being able to manage inventory to forecasted growth.

3. Do you have flexible operations?

We'll go into more detail, but Amazon has some shipping requirements that may be different from your other customers. Your warehouse team must be able to apply custom labels to every box, prepare according to Amazon's unique standards, and ship orders within a timely manner (usually three days or less).

Additionally, every product that you send to Amazon must be barcoded. This means that it either has a UPC printed on it when it's made or your warehouse team must be able to apply stickers manually to each product before a shipment goes out.

That's it. If your company can meet these three prerequisites, you can do it—you are ready to build your Amazon business.

What if you fall short on one or more of these? Not all is lost. As long as you have a right to win, you can make progress with Amazon. You may need to partner with a company that specializes in Amazon operations to handle your fulfillment. You can proceed with everything in this book and grow a substantial business while leaving the operational lift to a third party. For some of our clients, this is the way to go, as it lets them prove the channel out. And once the channel is large, it's a lot easier to make a business case for major operational changes.

The great news is that if you can check the boxes on these three requirements, I can guarantee you will be successful on Amazon!

Now that we got that out of the way, let's dive into the strategic framework that will guide you in how to build and grow your Amazon business.

The Amazon Strategic Framework: The Framework Guaranteed to Drive Massive Year-over-Year Growth in Your Amazon Business

I'm hyping this framework because it produces, and we apply it to each of our clients. It can be used by companies at any stage—from those that have never sold on Amazon to those with ten years of experience.

We've applied it to small manufacturers that do six figures a year and to large manufacturers that do six figures a day.

It not only offers guidance when thinking about your business overall but also works when looking at how to grow a specific product.

Sounds pretty great, right? It is. But the reason it's so great is because it's 100 percent based on how Amazon works—their flywheel. We covered this in chapter 3, and this same flywheel can be used to inform how to work with Amazon.

The following version of the Amazon flywheel includes the additional element of exactly what *you* need to do to make the flywheel operate in your favor:

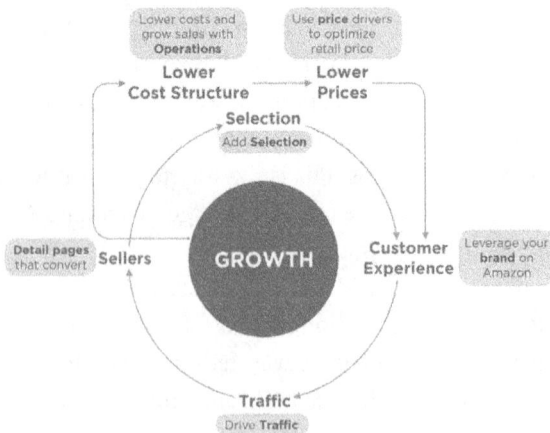

Simply put, Amazon gives you, as the manufacturer, the tools to positively impact how your products are treated at each element of the flywheel. Think of Amazon as the infrastructure provider. They provide manufacturers with tools and opportunities to lower cost structure, but you, as a savvy manufacturer, must take advantage of them.

That is why this framework succeeds so well. It's exactly how Amazon works, and they have tools, opportunities, and processes to help enable each of these elements for manufacturers of every size and every stage of business.

Here are the key elements we discuss in the rest of the book:

- *Price drivers:* Amazon is a very price-sensitive marketplace. They incentivize low prices and actively try to reduce their own margin and your margin too. The winning strategy is to optimize retail pricing to offer a competitive price while maintaining your margins. We share how to do this in chapter 6.

- *Operations:* Amazon is an operationally focused company. They will push your capabilities to the maximum, but the opportunity for you is to use your operations to lower costs and drive incremental sales. See chapter 7.

- *Detail pages that convert:* The listing pages are where people ultimately make the decision to buy (or not buy) your product. You want the pages to present your products effectively and to give them the best chance to be purchased. We explain the most critical elements impacting conversion in chapter 8.

- *Traffic:* Your pages only generate sales if people see them. Chapter 9 explains how to drive more and more traffic to your products.

These four key strategies are a major focus for the rest of the book, and a separate chapter is devoted to each of them. The last two framework elements do not have their own chapters, as we consider them to be more advanced topics. That said, they are worth briefly discussing.

Branding is a key strategy that enhances the effectiveness of your conversion and traffic initiatives. Strong branding is successful when everything else is working and can turn good results into great results. Focusing on it too early or when you have fundamental issues is probably more distracting than useful. That's why we're not covering it in this book.

Selection is another important key strategy. In its simplest form, it means adding as much of your catalog as possible to Amazon. We would strongly recommend this, as you never know exactly how much demand is out there. Virtually every one of our clients has a surprise bestseller on Amazon that they would never have guessed based on their non-Amazon sales. And the easiest way to discover all your bestsellers is to add your entire catalog.

After including your standard catalog, the focus should remain on the four other strategies—price, operations, conversion, and traffic. There are more advanced selection opportunities (pack sizes, packaging optimization, bundles, new products, etc.), but those are more advanced topics best tackled after the basics are under control.

The framework covers the strategies and activities that will make your business successful on Amazon. It's what you need to do to win. Before we go into the details of exactly what manufacturers should do in each of those areas, it's important to briefly talk about how manufacturers can work with Amazon.

If you don't have a relationship with Amazon, one of the first choices you need to make is how to engage with them. The next section outlines the two different ways that manufacturers can sell on Amazon.

Amazon's Two Selling Models

This section is primarily for the Amazon virgins—manufacturers that do not have any relationship with Amazon and, secondarily, manufacturers that are struggling with Amazon and thinking of quitting. If you are in either of these extremes, then thinking about how you sell on Amazon is important.

If you already have a relationship with Amazon and things are going great, OK, or even sort of OK, then you can skip this section. No need to revisit your selling model.

For the virgins and the companies about to swear off Amazon and go into celibacy, one decision you need to look at is your selling model.

There are two primary ways to do business on Amazon. The first is as a vendor. Vendors sell their products to Amazon, and Amazon resells them to customers.

A vendor relationship is a traditional manufacturer-retailer relationship. Amazon is responsible for buying inventory and selling it to end buyers. Amazon sets the retail price and is responsible if they stockout or get stuck with dead inventory. Most manufacturers are very comfortable with this selling model.

Products sold through a vendor relationship have Sold by Amazon labels on their product pages.

The second selling model is as a seller. Sellers sell their products directly to Amazon customers and use Amazon as a marketplace.

In this model, the seller is responsible for managing inventory and selling it (through Amazon) to the end buyer. The seller sets the retail price and needs to manage inventory so that they don't stockout or get stuck with dead inventory. The seller potentially gets a higher margin, as they are technically the retailer and get retail margins. However, they also take on inventory risk, returns, and certain customer service issues.

Products sold by sellers show Sold by XYZ Corp labels on their product pages. Assuming they have retail capabilities, there is nothing preventing a manufacturer from being a seller on Amazon.

It's worth sharing all the major differences between sellers and vendors:

	Amazon Retail Vendor		Seller (Third Party)	
	Purchase Order (PO)	Direct Fulfillment (DF)	Merchant Fulfillment Network (MFN)	Fulfilled By Amazon (FBA)
Retail Pricing	Amazon sets sell price based on market		Seller sets retail price	
Inventory	Amazon owned & managed, stored in Amazon FC	Vendor owned & managed, ships direct from Vendor to customer	Seller owned & managed	Seller owned & managed but stored in Amazon FC
Customer Data	Amazon doesn't share customer data	Customer name and address shown on ship to label	Customer data is known to seller*	
Costs	Deduction from invoice for basic terms and any chargebacks	Amazon pays freight to customer, normal COOP deductions apply	Seller pays a referral fee and for shipment to customer	Seller pays referral fee, fulfillment, storage and any chargebacks
Channel Conflict	Amazon is the retailer		Seller is retailer & competes directly against other sellers and other retailers	
Customer Trust	Ships from and sold by Amazon		Ships from and sold by Seller	Ships by Amazon and Sold by Seller
Amazon Rules	Prime eligible and search rank advantage		Not eligible for Prime**	Prime eligible and search rank advantage
Scannable Barcode	Required on each saleable unit	Not Required	Not Required	Required on each saleable unit

The cost structure varies as well:

Vendor PO	Vendor DF	Merchant Fulfillment Network (MFN)	Fulfilled By Amazon (FBA)
Amazon deducts from invoice for: PO Quick Pay (2 percent 30 Net 60)* CO-OP (8 percent)* Freight Allowance (inbound shipping) (5 percent)* Damage Allowance (2 percent)* Chargebacks for noncompliance Ala Carte Marketing Packages (Amazon pays for Shipment to Customer)	Amazon deducts from invoice for: PO Quick Pay (2 percent 30 Net 60)* CO-OP (8 percent)* Damage Allowance (2 percent)* Chargebacks for noncompliance Ala Carte Marketing Packages (AmaOzon pays for Shipment to Customer)	Amazon charges a referral fee based on the total cost (12-15 percent) Seller is responsible for shipping to end customer	Amazon charges a referral fee based on the total cost (12-15 percent) Fulfillment Fee** Storage** ** size and weight based

* Sample terms only. ** Based on size, weight, and product type.

Supply chain options vary as well:

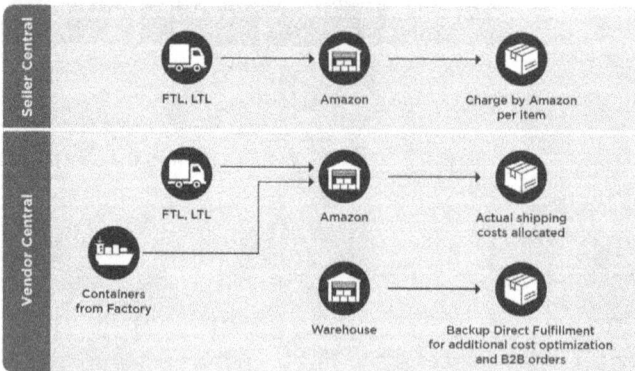

There are a lot of details we're glossing over, but from a supply chain perspective, vendors have more options to scale as they grow.

At the end of the day, the most important thing to know is that both models can be successful and profitable. Manufacturers can succeed as a vendor or as a seller.

Anyone telling you otherwise is trying to sell you something. (Most likely, services will switch from one to another.) Although there are sometimes good reasons to transfer and sometimes one is easier than the other, the benefits of switching are often oversold by Amazon consulting companies.

They will tout all the advantages of being a seller (and coincidentally work only with sellers). A quick Google search on this topic will return dozens of results. However, most of the information you find on the internet is written by consultants who are trying to get vendors to become sellers. Do not trust it!

You might be asking yourself, *Well, why should I trust you?* After all, I own a firm that sells Amazon services. How am I any different from the random companies telling you to switch?

The answer is pretty simple. We don't sell a one-size-fits-all approach. We sell Amazon expertise. We have deep experience helping manufacturers succeed with Amazon using both vendor and seller models. Our goal is to make you as successful as possible, and it's rare that the selling model is the primary reason for success or failure.

We mention this because we are frequently asked this question—whether moving from vendor to seller can turn an Amazon business around. Most of the time the answer is no.

So if you are already a seller or a vendor, most likely stick with it. However, if you have no relationship with Amazon, you do need to choose one. The following checklists highlight some of the biggest factors that go into that decision.

Being a vendor is a better selling method if you meet these criteria:

- You have stable pricing for your customers and not a lot of price fluctuations.
- You primarily sell wholesale or B2B and do not have a significant DTC business.

- Your sales volume potential has the ability to make you a top twenty vendor in your category. This would mean having a path to at least seven figures a year in less competitive categories and eight figures in more competitive markets.
- Your products are already on Amazon with established demand.
- Your other customers would be upset if they saw your products being sold directly to end users as a retailer.
- You sell products in an underserved Amazon market.
- You are able to get access to the vendor platform.

Being an Amazon seller might be a better option if you meet the following criteria:

- You are already on Vendor Central and it's not profitable *and* you've tried everything in this book.
- Your company is experienced in DTC selling and is comfortable with providing customer service and handling returns.
- Your retail customers would not be upset to see your products sold directly on Amazon.
- Your costs and market pricing fluctuate significantly or are unpredictable.

Like we said, there is a lot of misleading information out there, and manufacturers can be successful on either platform. If you have any questions or want to discuss the specifics of your business, we'd be happy to talk you through the options at no charge.

Now that you have a selling model to get your products on the Amazon platform, it's time to dive into the strategic framework. The first area we'll cover is pricing.

CHAPTER 6

PRODUCT PRICING: HOW TO GET WINNING MARGINS, MOTIVATE AMAZON TO SELL YOUR PRODUCTS, AND GIVE BUYERS A GREAT VALUE

P ricing is the most important factor in winning on Amazon. Price too low and you'll destroy your profit margin. You might get the sales volume, but your profitability will be poor. Price too high and your margins will be great but no one will buy your product.

Pricing is broken into two parts—wholesale pricing for vendors and retail pricing, which is for sellers and vendors. You may think that if you are a vendor and wholesaling product to Amazon that you don't need to worry about retail pricing. This could not be more wrong. The retail price determines your sales volume—for both sellers and vendors—as that is what buyers see and make decisions on.

Sellers can skip the wholesale pricing section, but vendors need to study both the wholesale and the retail sections. They must correctly set wholesale prices to ensure profitability and then optimize retail prices to ensure volume.

Wholesale Pricing to Amazon: The Most Important Section of This Book if You Are a Vendor

Let me repeat—wholesale pricing is the single most important concept to understand in this book. Because if vendors do it wrong, they can sabotage their long-term success. Unfortunately, many do it wrong, and it is extremely difficult to fix.

The root issue comes from falsehood #1 in chapter 2—believing that Amazon is like your other customers. Manufacturers think in terms of wholesale price lists and price tiers. They make the mistake of giving Amazon standard wholesale pricing. If you do that, there is a good chance you are leaving money on the table and risking your Amazon business in the future!

Amazon is not like your other customers. Your other customers are likely humans who have ideas about what a product should cost. Amazon is an algorithm that treats your product like every other. You want to price your products in a way that makes the most sense to Amazon's algorithm.

Amazon's pricing algorithm is designed to measure Amazon's product profitability. If Amazon can sell the product profitably, it's happy with your price.

In other words, Amazon does not expect a standard discount. It looks at the costs to sell each product individually and whether it can source the product profitability.

For example, Amazon sells a lot of different watches. They have models for $20 and for over $1,000. The interesting thing is that regardless of whether the watch is $20 or $1,000, it costs Amazon approximately the same amount to pick, pack, and ship the watch to the end customer.

If it costs Amazon $10 to ship a watch, their gross margin changes dramatically depending on the watch's selling price. Amazon spends 50 percent of the price to ship a $20 watch but spends only 1 percent to ship a $1,000 watch.

If you were a watch manufacturer, Amazon might not want to sell your $20 watch if you sold it to them for 50 percent off list. But they would gladly sell your $1,000 watch for 50 percent off list. And if you did that, you would be giving away a tremendous amount of margin because Amazon would probably gladly sell that $1,000 watch for only 10 percent off list.

Amazon has more scale and cost efficiency than your other customers. As a result, they are willing to sell your products for less margin than your other customers.

Here is a real example from one of our clients. They wholesale their products at 48 percent off list. Amazon's margin requirements always depend on the product specifics, but for this example, we'll use an average. For this client, Amazon's average margin must be at least 35 percent.

(Keep in mind that all examples here are simplifications. We do not take into account deductions, product specifics, or other details that impact Amazon's actual costs.)

One of their products lists for $100. Because of this, our client would normally charge Amazon $52 for the product (48 percent off list).

But because Amazon needs only a 35 percent margin, our client could charge Amazon up to $65 and Amazon would still be happy. Instead of selling the product to Amazon for $52, they can sell it to Amazon for $65 and Amazon would still buy.

That $13 difference goes straight to profit. And in our client's case, it increases their profit margin on this product by over 30 percent! This strategy has made Amazon their most profitable account.

Alternatively, they could have made the decision to pass some of the $13 onto the end buyers through a lower retail price. In that case, they would have decreased their profit margin but increased their product demand with a lower retail price point.

The worst outcome would be giving the $13 to Amazon. That scenario is great for Amazon but does nothing for your company's profitability or for the end buyer.

You are probably wondering how we knew Amazon needed only a 35 percent margin on our client's products. Over the years, we've built a model that estimates Amazon's costs at the product level. It takes into account the primary cost drivers and estimates Amazon's costs based on that.

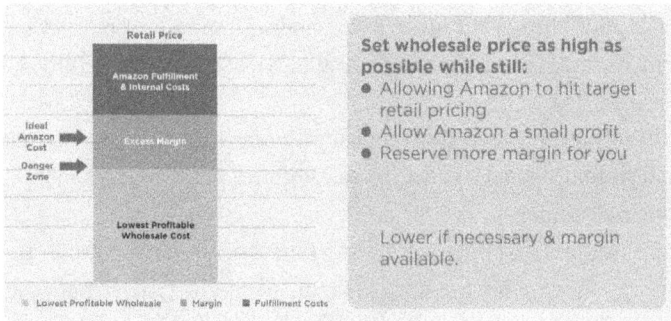

You can build your own costing model to estimate Amazon's expected margins with your products using Amazon's FBA calculator—a tool that estimates Amazon's fees to sell a product as a seller. Amazon's vendor side of the business operates on lower margins than the seller side. The seller fee calculator gives a good conservative estimate of how much it costs Amazon to fulfill a product.

When building out a full cost model, you'll want to take into account all the major cost drivers within Amazon. These include overhead, inbound shipping, Amazon internal profitability requirements, and returns.

The wholesale price sets your profit margin and is a key factor in Amazon's profitability. The best wholesale price is one where you have a great margin and Amazon has enough profitability to want to continue to sell your products.

But Amazon's profitability isn't determined by wholesale price alone. They have several costs that you must account for such as overhead and shipping to the end customer, to name just two. And the most important remaining factor in determining Amazon's profitability (and whether your product sells at all) is the retail price. We cover what you need to know about retail pricing in the next section.

Retail Pricing on Amazon: Critical for Sellers and Vendors

If you are a seller on Amazon, you are responsible for setting the retail price, and it's probably the single most important decision to make. If you are a vendor, Amazon is responsible for retail pricing. But vendors need to focus just as much on retail pricing as sellers.

This doesn't come naturally to all manufacturers. Some manufacturers have minimum advertised price (MAP) policies and strong positions on retail pricing. They actively police retailers to ensure that retail pricing is enforced. But many manufacturers focus just on making and selling at wholesale and leave retail pricing up to their customers.

Whether you care about retail pricing for your goods or not, it is a critical component to be successful on Amazon. There are three reasons why this is true.

First, your retail price is a huge factor in a shopper's buying decision. If your retail price is too expensive, you will lose the majority of your sales. Amazon's website brings a large amount of transparency to pricing, and shoppers respond. There are many markets where, if the retail pricing is only 5 to 10 percent too high, sales will drop to zero. However, if your products are good values for their price relative to other products on Amazon, you can win.

Second, other retailers price check Amazon's prices. The retail price on Amazon is not only extremely visible to Amazon shoppers but also extremely visible to your other channels and customers. If Amazon (or you) is pricing your bestselling product extremely low, you can upset your other customers who may not be able to profitably match Amazon.

Conversely, Amazon price checks other retailers. If you price too high and your products are not competitive relative to other strategic retailers, Amazon will penalize your product pages and you will lose sales.

Third, if you are a vendor, retail pricing directly affects Amazon's profitability. Selling on Amazon is a partnership. It needs to be profitable for you and for Amazon. If the retail pricing on Amazon is too low, Amazon can lose money on your products.

73

This sounds like a crazy scenario, but it happens regularly. The reason is that Amazon is a retail price follower. They scrape the internet for product pricing and try to match the lowest price for your products—even if doing so causes them to lose money. Amazon is willing to lose money in the short term, but if they lose money for too long, they will stop selling your products, and this will kill your progress on Amazon.

For these reasons, you want your products to have retail pricing that ensures you are competitive in the marketplace, that you do not upset your other customers and channels, and that is profitable for Amazon. This can be a delicate balance, but it is the key to pricing successfully.

Successful retail pricing is pricing that lets Amazon make some money and that gives a good value to buyers and a great margin to you. Once you know where that pricing is, you can reverse engineer a wholesale cost to Amazon (if you are a vendor). In many cases, this is significantly more than what you would charge them as a more typical wholesale customer.

And if you are a seller, this all still applies. Sellers have the advantage of directly setting the market price. However, Amazon will penalize your sales if the price is not market competitive. Although as a seller you do not need to worry about Amazon's profitability, you do need to worry about Amazon's fees and your profitability.

Pricing analysis can get extremely complex. If you do not have the resources to do a full analysis, we would recommend a test-and-adjust approach. Create pricing bands for your retail and wholesale prices. Start the pricing a bit higher than you might otherwise and then lower them if you get signals that they are too high. Vendors can always lower costs but cannot raise them easily. Sellers can easily raise or lower costs (though there is a limit on how much prices can be increased per month).

Correct Pricing Creates a Win-Win-Win Situation

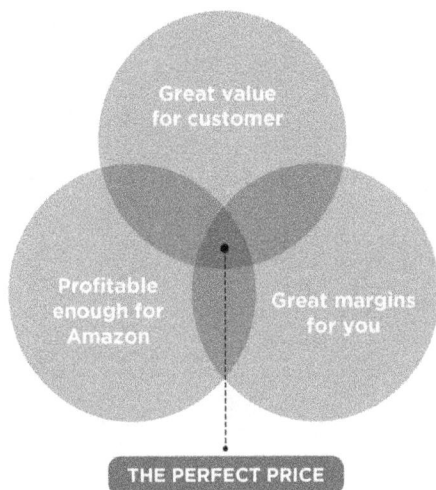

Great value for customer

Profitable enough for Amazon

Great margins for you

THE PERFECT PRICE

The goal of pricing is to find the sweet spot—a good margin for you, a good value for the buyer, and a sufficient margin for Amazon. A good margin for you makes a healthy and happy business, now and into the future. A good value for buyers maximizes their demand for your products. A sufficient margin for Amazon ensures that they will continue to want to sell your products. Achieving this triple win supercharges sales.

Got all that? It's a lot for one chapter, and we have more pricing best practices to discuss next, but we'll treat pricing as a subtopic of operations rather than as the main event.

See you in chapter 7.

CHAPTER 7

HOW TO PLUG AMAZON INTO YOUR BUSINESS AND LIGHT UP YOUR REVENUE (WITHOUT BURNING UP OPERATIONS)

Your products' prices guarantee profit—or guarantee your business *won't* be profitable. It's the single-most important driver of success on Amazon.

The second most important step is ensuring that your products are in stock and available for sale. Sounds simple. But staying in stock at scale can be a challenge. This is where your operations come in. Your Amazon business success depends on your operations ability to execute and scale in Amazon's own peculiar way.

True Operational Excellence Drives Sales on Amazon

Operational excellence is critical to succeeding on Amazon. Outside of a right to win (of which pricing is a big part), the ability to execute operationally is the biggest factor in your success or failure with Amazon.

Many companies claim to have good operations, and if your company is successful and has been around for a while, you likely do. But what I'm talking about here is operational excellence at an Amazon level. If you are not able to efficiently and reliably feed the Amazon flywheel, you will lose sales, increase both your and Amazon's costs, lose momentum, and strengthen your competition. Just as the flywheel creates a positive feedback loop to grow sales, bad operations create a negative feedback loop that can destroy your Amazon business.

None of the other strategies or tactics in this book are as important to growing your Amazon business as being able to ship on time and reliably and according to Amazon's requirements. Amazon-level operations are key.

Operations make the difference between good and great sales performance. Most companies think of operations as a cost center. For Amazon, your operations can drive sales as much as your sales and marketing efforts. Efficient and responsive supply chains drive growth on Amazon. It all goes back to Amazon's flywheel.

As such, it's critical that your organization understands and masters Amazon's requirements. Amazon has detailed documentation, requirements, and training that are available in their supplier portals. Your team must go through all of it and understand it in detail. Amazon does a great job of explaining the requirements, so there's no need to rehash them here.

But it is worth covering their requirements at a strategic level. Amazon's operational requirements will impact your organization in five areas:

1. Order management
2. Product preparation and labeling
3. Order fulfillment
4. Forecasting
5. Monitoring performance

Order management is the process of receiving, accepting, and completing orders to payment. This can be done manually or electronically via EDI or API. The details of the process depend on whether you are a seller or a vendor, but it is worth noting that handling orders manually will quickly become time-consuming. Amazon generates a lot of orders.

Additionally, manual order processing increases the risk of errors, and Amazon has severe penalties when it comes to errors. Manual order processing is recommended only when you are starting and sales volume is relatively slow.

Product preparation and labeling are processes meant to ensure that Amazon can receive and inventory your products efficiently and safely. First is product labeling. Amazon receives products in a highly automated way, and to make that happen, every product must be barcoded with a UPC, a GTIN, or an EAN.

The barcode is how Amazon identifies the item. If your products do not have a barcode, a barcode label will need to be manually applied to each item before it ships.

Many retailers receive products manually or have receivers that can identify products. Not true with Amazon. Amazon uses the barcode exclusively to identify products.

Labeling is extremely critical, as it is the only way that Amazon can accurately receive your product. If you send in a product that is missing barcodes, it will eventually be manually reviewed. But there is a significant chance it will get received incorrectly or lost, and if that happens, you will not get paid for it.

Second, products should be sent in such a way that they can be immediately shipped out to a customer or stored safely. Amazon must make sure that normal handling will not damage the product, other products in the same bin, or the people processing it. And Amazon needs to be confident that the product can handle shipping without damage.

If your products do not come in their own six-sided boxes, then there is a chance they will require some preparation before being sent to Amazon. Prep can include putting it in a polybag, wrapping it in bubble wrap, or other steps depending on the product. Amazon will do this but charges you for the service.

Order fulfillment is the process of shipping items to Amazon. I want to highlight a couple of requirements here:

- *Shipping speed:* Amazon's flywheel depends on rapid replenishment. You should be able to ship products in under a week in all cases, and certain types of orders require one to two days from order receipt to shipment.

- *Carton contents:* Amazon needs to know the contents of each shipping carton it receives from you to help receive products more efficiently. This means that every shipping carton requires barcoding, and the carton contents must be communicated back to Amazon. This is an extra step for many shipping teams and mandates some specific training.

Forecasting is the process of ensuring that you have product in your warehouse and in Amazon's warehouse. I bring this up because the parabolic nature of Amazon sales can cause sudden stockouts.

I have a client who manufactures overseas with a four-month lead time. They had stable demand from their existing channels and held ample inventory in the US to support that demand. The company already sold products to Amazon with little success when we started working with them. When they hired us, we were able to fix their root issues in the first six months and sales took off—causing them to stockout.

They suddenly couldn't fill orders for their other customers, let alone the demand on Amazon. They doubled their normal orders back to the factory. It took four months for the replacement stock to arrive. Once it did, they almost immediately stocked out again. This process repeated itself five times before they reached their new, much larger stock levels to support both Amazon and their other customers. It took them two years to get to a new steady-state level of inventory (and during that time, their Amazon sales increased tenfold.)

This is an extreme example, but it illustrates how demand swings on Amazon can be very outsized compared to your other channels and can suddenly spike once you are successful. Managing your inventory and forecasting demand are critical.

If you are a vendor with Amazon, they will provide you a forecast on the number of units they project they will sell. This does a decent job of predicting steady-state demand but underforecasts growing demand. If you are a seller on their platform, you are responsible for forecasting demand, and Amazon provides some reporting to help with that. This process can be a bit more complex, as you not only need to manage inventory levels in your warehouse(s) but also manage inventory at Amazon. The way we solve this is to build a forecasting model. A good Amazon forecasting model includes Amazon-specific growth factors and takes into account point-of-sale demand rather than just historical sales. If you stockout frequently, your past sales may be a fraction of the true demand.

As with all things with Amazon, the key to operational excellence is to focus on the fundamental requirements and to continue to improve and scale over time. Set the goal of being able to operate at an Amazon level of operational excellence and make ongoing improvements. This will enable you not only to scale as your Amazon business grows but also to give a higher level of service to your other customers.

A key part of improvement is measuring performance, and we cover that in the next section.

Monitoring Operational Performance So That You Can Manage It

The great thing about operations is that not only is it a major growth driver but also operational metrics are some of the easiest performance metrics to track (right after sales).

The adage that you can't improve what you don't measure is very true in e-commerce and in operations in particular. And because operations are so important for Amazon, they provide you with tons of data that can track your operational performance.

The first place to regularly monitor your operational performance is via Amazon's dashboards in their portal.

Vendors have the following:

- *Operational performance:* See where Amazon has identified issues with your inbound shipments.
- *Direct fulfillment report:* Monitor your drop-ship performance.

Both of these reports will highlight issues that are costing you money in charge-backs. Charge-backs are areas of operational friction and can indirectly impact sales. The goal is to have zero charge-backs.

Sellers have the following:

- *Account health:* Monitor product, shipment, and order issues all in one place.
- *Inventory planning, inventory performance, and restocking reports:* Monitor your inventory at Amazon.
- *Shipment performance:* Track defects on inventory sent to Amazon.

We recommend monitoring these dashboards weekly and performing root cause analysis on any trends or recurring issues.

Additionally, there are several metrics that must be tracked outside of the dashboards:

- *Order cancellations:* Vendor orders need to be canceled if you do not have the product in stock. Management is often not aware of how much sales opportunity is lost due to cancellations by their customer service teams.
- *Shortages:* Shortages can be an issue for both vendors and sellers. It is critical to track how much product is lost—shipped but not received.
- *On-time shipments:* Vendors see if their inbound shipments are late in their dashboard, but sellers should maintain a weekly or biweekly shipping schedule into Amazon's fulfillment centers.

All these are early-warning signs that you are losing sales or eroding your margin. Every growing company will occasionally have issues here, but the goal for operational excellence is zero order cancellations, zero shortages, and 100 percent on-time shipments.

You also need to monitor the inventory levels at Amazon.

Vendors must ensure that Amazon maintains sufficient inventory of their products. You might assume that Amazon has it handled. They usually do, but when they don't, you need to be ready to step in. We've seen many instances where Amazon doesn't always buy enough or stops buying altogether and would let their inventory go out of stock if you do not intercede. You should track the weeks of cover that are inbound and in stock and take action if it falls too low.

Sellers must make sure the inventory is just right as well. If you have too little inventory at Amazon, you risk going out of stock. If you have too few shipments going to Amazon, you risk going out of stock if one (or more) gets delayed. On the flip side, if you send too much inventory, you will end up paying too much to store it. It's a delicate balancing act that requires active management.

Finally, you should monitor that your products are actually listed for sale. Just because there is inventory available does not guarantee that your products will be live on the website and being actively sold. Glitches in Amazon's backend, compliance issues, and unauthorized sellers are just a few potential causes that could prevent in-stock products from being sold.

This can be done manually by checking key listings every few days, or it can be done via software. At the end of the day, having a product out of stock or not available for sale impacts your top and bottom lines much more than Amazon's. Checking to ensure that your product is offered for sale is a cheap insurance policy that protects your sales.

Tracking these key metrics will give you targets for improvement and confirm that your operations are in order. Now that Amazon can receive and sell your products, the last step in incorporating Amazon into your business is ensuring that they and your other sales channels can coexist happily.

Addressing Channel Management Concerns: Best Practices

As a manufacturer, you may be concerned with pricing across your sales channels. For example, you might want to ensure that all your retailers have a fair opportunity to sell your products. Or your products are premium, and pricing accordingly is a key strategy. Amazon is a big and highly visible retailer, so it's important that they sell your products in a way that doesn't disrupt your existing retail customers and so that your other retail customers do not jeopardize your full potential on Amazon.

Please note that we can only provide general advice here. We're always happy to discuss the specifics of your situation. What follows are some of the most common perceived and real issues that we encounter in our advising.

Complaints and Conflicts from Existing Customers

"If I sell on Amazon, all my existing customers will drop my product line." Or: "Amazon will sell my products so low, my other retailers will all start calling me to complain because they won't be able to compete."

This can be a big concern for manufacturers. They value their existing customers and do not want to upset them by selling on Amazon.

The reality we see is that, more often than not, manufacturers do not get a ton of complaints from their other retail customers when they launch on Amazon. Most retailers, the good ones at least, have learned to live (and often thrive) in an Amazon world.

It is worth noting that the *fear* of complaints from existing customers is often greater than the *reality* of complaints from existing customers. Launching, in itself, rarely causes issues with your other customers.

A second reason that having an Amazon presence rarely causes conflict is that the Amazon customer is often different from your other customers' customers. The actual, direct competition between them and Amazon may be less than you originally would guess.

However, you can expect to get calls if Amazon starts to undercut their retail pricing. It can be an issue when Amazon sells products below the cost that your other retailers can even purchase them for. As we discussed in chapter 6, Amazon will sell for a loss to be market competitive. In other words, as a price follower, Amazon will match the lowest product price they see online.

When this happens, it's not really an Amazon issue; it's a market price issue. The best way to handle this is to actively manage your channels and work with your resellers to ensure that everyone has a chance to make money. Additionally, you can always cut off the low-price competitor—or Amazon, if you cannot resolve the issue. We recommend minimizing the potential of this happening by having a smart pricing strategy that makes it unprofitable for Amazon (and others) to discount significantly. Doing this doesn't guarantee that Amazon won't discount if your other channels do, but it generally ensures that Amazon won't initiate a price war.

If cross-channel complaints or conflicts are a concern for your business, we recommend a test-and-see approach to determine how significant an issue it actually is. Usually it's minimal, but if it's significant, it can be dealt with. Either way, test and see is better than not proceeding at all. Especially because the complaints and issues often never materialize.

Minimum Advertised Pricing (MAP) Policies

MAP policies are a good way to help maintain market prices. A MAP for your products ensures that all retailers have a fair chance at making enough margin by preventing any retailer from advertising below a specific minimum.

If all your retailers follow MAP, so will Amazon.

It is important to understand that Amazon always follows market pricing. If all retailers behave, so does Amazon. But if Amazon sees other retailers selling for less than MAP, they will follow and discount as well.

This market price concept applies even if you are a seller who can set your own retail price. Although Amazon cannot make you lower your market price, they can punish you for not being competitive (from their perspective). If competitor retailers are selling for less than MAP, and you as a seller do not match that retail price, Amazon will suppress your listing and redirect traffic to products they feel are more competitively priced.

The key factor in having a MAP policy is enforcement. If you do not punish your retailers who violate MAP, you effectively do not have MAP.

Amazon really highlights whether you do a good job of enforcing MAP. If you have a couple of bad actors, you risk Amazon finding them and matching their price. And once that happens, you can count on all your retailers noticing.

Because of this, monitoring your MAP policy is key. You want to find violations before Amazon magnifies the impact. There are many services out there that will help you enforce MAP, and it's even a service we do with respect to maintaining prices on Amazon.

Online Reseller Agreements

Online reseller agreements go hand in hand with MAP policies. They are a contractual way of preventing unauthorized online sales.

We believe that reseller agreements are a critical component for most manufacturers' e-commerce strategies. The reason is that there are two types of online retailers.

The first type of retailer, which we describe in this book, is developing an online business that is sustainable and reaches new markets. They recognize that customers want to interact online, so they try to offer the best experience possible. This means providing customer service and translating your brand and the value you deliver into the online world. This type of business adds to your existing business and ensures that your business continues to grow as buying trends evolve.

The second type of online retailer is a reseller who is an online middleman. They are willing to sacrifice brand equity for short-term gain. They are arbitraging across channels to make a sliver of profit. In the process, they destroy margins for other retailers and provide no added value to you or to the end buyer. Once the profitability of your products has dried up, they move onto something else.

Unfortunately, there are a lot of these second types of online retailers out there. They may occasionally place a nice order with your company, but they do not add any value. And if you follow the recommendations in this book, not only do you not need them but also you will not want their business. You will instead have developed a more direct beneficial channel through Amazon that increases your sales and makes your end users happier.

And that is where online reseller agreements come in. They can help prevent these companies from sourcing and reselling your products. You allow the first type of retailers to sell and cut out the second type.

Like with MAP policies, online reseller agreements require active monitoring to ensure compliance. For Amazon specifically, this involves scanning to see who is selling your products and confirming that they are authorized resellers.

The goal of this chapter was to explain how to plug Amazon into your business. The biggest internal point of interface with Amazon will be through your operations team. Their ability to execute is the single greatest nonproduct factor in your success. We discussed in detail key ways to monitor operational success.

Adding Amazon to your business also impacts your other channels of distribution. We covered the most common channel-related concerns, and these fears are usually manageable.

You have officially passed the prerequisite phase. You are aware of what you need to know about Amazon and the requirements necessary to succeed. Now it's time to focus on exactly what you must do to grow your Amazon business—and scale your products all the way to the top of the bestseller charts.

CHAPTER 8

HOW A VIRTUAL SALESPERSON WILL MAKE YOUR PAGES CONVERT LIKE CRAZY

Up until now, we've discussed only how to engage with Amazon and integrate it into your business. The primary focus has been the impact Amazon will have on your business so that you are prepared. Those steps are critical prerequisites to success and ensure that once your products start selling, you have the necessary horsepower behind them to ramp up sales in a pain-free way. Ramping up sales ramps up your profits. All that is what you need to know to win.

But now we'll cover exactly what you need to do to ramp up those sales. To make your products bestsellers on Amazon. This is usually the easier part—after all, Amazon's platform is designed to connect buyers with the best products. And you have the best products because you have a right to win. But to ensure that win on the platform, you need to know the correct levers to pull to get the Amazon flywheel to start doing its magic.

I've mentioned this before, but it's useful to think of Amazon as a machine. Once you learn how to operate it, it can produce reliable and repeatable results.

This chapter (and the next) applies to both new and existing products. When you add a new product, you want to set it up properly to win. These chapters will outline what you need to do to make your products winners from day one.

But you may already have your entire catalog on Amazon, and many products may already be selling. These chapters apply here as well.

It's common to find hidden gems in a company's catalog. A hidden gem is a product that deserves to be a bestseller (i.e., have a right to win) but that, for some reason, is not selling well. It's a gem that hasn't been found yet. Most likely hidden gems are missing one or two key ingredients. Add the missing ingredient, and sales skyrocket.

This chapter also applies to current bestsellers. There is almost always room for improvement. At Mantaro Partners, we believe improvement is a continuous process. You make more progress (i.e., more sales/profit) by incorporating a series of sequential changes versus one big set of changes. You learn more as you go, and each change improves on the last. Each improvement could open a new opportunity, or give you new information, or cause a change in the marketplace overall.

In short, improving your Amazon business is an ongoing, iterative process. Amazon is growing fast and is highly dynamic, so there are always new opportunities.

This is the essence of the thinking that bestsellers are made, not born. If you start with a strong right to win, you just need to take the correct steps and let Amazon do its magic with the flywheel.

In fact, this optimization process is a virtuous cycle too: the flywheel brings success, which opens up new opportunities, which can bring more success!

The best part of this process is that with Amazon's winner-takes-most market dynamic, the bestseller in a niche can take a disproportionate amount of the sales for the niche. This means that your sales and growth on a bestseller can be five to ten times or more than an average product.

You can't make a bestseller directly by negotiating with Amazon. But you can create an environment that encounters a product to become a bestseller. You do this by focusing on the key inputs—the things that you can control—and trust the flywheel to handle the key outputs (sales).

The way that you make a bestseller is to focus on the key inputs that impact whether customers buy your product. The inputs relate to two key factors, conversion and traffic, and they contribute to the key output sales. Simply, it's this:

$$Sales = Conversion \times Traffic$$

Conversion is how well your product page converts visitors to buyers. Inputs that increase conversion drive sales by making your page a more effective virtual salesperson. You want your product pages to sell your products as best as they can. The better job they do, the more effective they are at converting traffic.

Traffic is how many visitors come to a product page. The second set of inputs have to do with traffic. The more traffic you send to your pages, the more sales you get.

Any conversion improvement drives a proportional increase in sales, and any traffic improvement also drives a proportional increase in sales. By focusing on both traffic and conversion, you get a multiplicative effect. If you can increase your conversion 30 percent and your traffic 30 percent, you don't get a 30 percent increase in sales—it increases sales by 70 percent!

It's even better than that. Often it takes only a tweak or two on specific inputs to increase your conversion or traffic by very large factors. When the flywheel kicks in, you can get an outsized result. It's not impossible to double sales with one change!

The rest of this chapter focuses on conversion, and chapter 9 covers everything you need to know to get traffic. Both chapters outline high-level principles and approaches to get you the most bang for your buck on Amazon (and likely on your other e-commerce channels as well). All these principles and tactics can be applied to both existing and new (to Amazon) products right now as well as on an ongoing basis into the future. After all—bestsellers are made, not born!

Conversion 101: Creating Your Virtual Salesperson

Conversion is the process of turning page visitors into buyers. As a measure, it assesses how good your pages are. The more likely a visitor buys after viewing your product pages, the better your pages are at converting.

The ultimate goal is to have your pages act as your virtual salesperson. You want to have them communicate your products' benefits and convince the visitor to buy as well as you could if talking to a customer face-to-face.

You may not achieve a virtual salesperson-level page on day one . . . or on day one hundred. A true virtual salesperson may require more resources than you have available today and may not even be possible (for a web page to be as good as you are).

If this concept seems daunting, don't get hung up on it too much. The real goal is continuous improvement, and using a virtual salesperson is the mindset you want when thinking about how to present your products on Amazon.

For example, when meeting with a prospect, a good virtual salesperson would discuss the following:

- Why buy the product

- Benefits/features
- Correct specifications
- Compatibility
- Superiority
- Cross-sells/upsells

It makes sense to include this type of content on product pages when available. And it probably makes sense to create content like this for better sellers. The more content like this that you can add, the higher the conversion and the more effective your virtual salesperson will be.

Minimum First-Step Requirements to Convert

Additionally, the first step toward that goal of a maximally converting page is much simpler.

The first step in conversion is making sure that three things are always true: your product is (1) *in stock* at Amazon, and (2) your product is *buyable* on Amazon at a (3) *good price*. In fact, as a reader of this book, you are most of the way there, as we've already covered the importance of having items in stock and the value of a good price.

If you are just starting out or have a small volume of sales, you can probably assume that if your product is in stock, then it is buyable. But it would be better to periodically check your listing pages to make sure that the product is being sold either by Amazon (if you are a vendor) or by you (if you are a seller). But as you grow, there will come a point when you will want to actively monitor the Amazon website to make sure the products you think are selling are actively being sold.

All this may seem extremely obvious, and to a degree it is. Despite that, these are easy first steps to overlook. If it turns out that your products are not in stock, not buyable, or are priced too high, nothing else in this section will work. And despite it being an obvious point, it is a very common problem with Amazon accounts that have not been actively managed.

Once the first step (in stock, buyable, good pricing) is confirmed, you are ready to start implementing your virtual salesperson. The next section explains exactly how to do that.

The Anatomy of a Listing Page

The listing page (a.k.a. the product detail page), which is the Amazon page that offers your product for sale, is the place where the sale for your product happens. Or not. The page, and the various components that Amazon lets you edit, is your virtual salesperson. It's the one thing on Amazon that you can control directly that shoppers use to make a decision to buy.

Your goal is to edit the listing page into the best virtual salesperson you can. You want the page to highlight the benefits your product provides and to address any potential concerns. The better job you do, the better the page will convert and the more sales you will get.

Product pages can have hundreds of fields listed in the backend, and the first time you see all the fields Amazon collects, it can be extremely daunting. Although it's best to provide Amazon with as much information as you can, that may not always be practical or possible.

Therefore, I wanted to share with you the content areas that I consider to be the most important for potential buyers. These are the content areas that buyers pay attention to the most and that, in our experience, have the biggest impact on conversion.

The Top Three Fields

Outside of price, the top three areas you have to sell your products are as follows:

1. Product title
2. Product images
3. Product bullets

The title, images, and bullets are the most critical content when it comes to Amazon. Outside of price, they are the top things consumers look at when deciding to buy. In many cases, these may be the only areas a customer looks at before adding the product to their cart or moving on.

Additionally, having relevant content in these sections positively impacts how the Amazon algorithm treats your listing. Good titles and bullets and a full set of high-resolution images will rank higher in search results than the same listing with less content.

For all these key fields, the important concept to remember is that buyers relate best to solutions and think in terms of benefits. They care much less about products or features because they are buying a solution, not a product, and they want to experience a benefit, not a feature.

For example, you may sell tree trimmers, but that is not what your customers are buying. They are buying a solution to make their trees look nice or to remove the branch too close to their patio. As such, you want the titles, images, and bullets to highlight the solutions—what customers can do with the product and how their life will be better rather than just stating product specifications.

Here are more specific recommendations for each of these three fields.

Titles

At a minimum, the product title should accurately describe the product. Amazon has category-specific guidelines, but generally all titles begin with the brand followed by a generic description of the product. If your brand is Razzor and you sell tree trimmers, at a minimum your product title should be *Razzor Tree Trimmer, 10 Ft.*

But this title doesn't really do your product justice. It's not descriptive and doesn't sell your product. Additionally, it's probably based on how you identify the product. It may not align with how people actually search for tree-trimming products.

Amazon provides up to two hundred characters to describe your item, and that gives you a chance to sell your product. A better title would be *Razzor Tree Trimmer Polesaw, 10 Foot Reach with Telescoping Handle, Tree Pruner for Branch Cutting.*

Someone searching for a tree trimmer would know from the title alone if the product might be a good fit for what they need. It includes the solution "branch cutting" as well as the clear features and benefits of "10 Foot Reach with Telescoping Handle," which helps with their buying decision.

Additionally, customers may use multiple different searches to find a tree trimmer. Whether they are searching for "tree trimmer," "polesaw," or "tree pruner," the title will resonate with them. A good title describes your product in your buyer's words.

Images

Although titles are the first thing people see on the page, they likely spend the most time browsing your product's images. Every shopper will check out at least your product's main images, and some shoppers will buy your product based 100 percent on images alone. You want your images not only to show your product but also to actively sell your product. Your images should give a visual representation of the benefits and the key messages of your product.

In the appendix, we include the image guidelines we share with our clients. Amazon allows six images to be displayed on the product page. You ideally want to use all six images per product, but you need at least one image for the product to be sellable. For manufacturers new to e-commerce, we would consider three images per product as a starting goal.

As a bare minimum requirement, the product images must accurately show the item and set a clear expectation for what the buyer will get.

The ideal goal, as we said, is for the images to actively sell the product. For that to happen, they need to communicate the item's unique features and benefits and how it is used.

This can be done in several ways. One is purely visually, with lifestyle images showing the product in use so that the potential buyer imagines themselves in the images using the product. It can be an infographic that summarizes a key message in text form, or it can be an annotated version of the product that calls out specific unique features.

There are dozens of different ways that images can be used to become your virtual salesperson. If you run out of inspiration, just browse your competitors' images or even completely different categories.

To use the tree trimmer example again, some potential images might include the following:

- The main image of the tree trimmer on a clean white background.
- A close-up of the telescoping feature, potentially with annotations to clearly show how it works.
- A lifestyle shot of a homeowner using the tree trimmer to cut a branch very high up.
- Another lifestyle close-up shot of the tree trimmer cutting a branch to really bring the value proposition to life.
- An image of the saw blade with an annotation showing how long the cutting edge is.
- A shot of the tree trimmer in its storage case to show it comes with a nice case.
- An infographic that shares your exceptional warranty.
- An infographic highlighting the maximum trimming height and that it is longer than the competition.

The next step would then be to reduce this list down to the top six images that tell the best story about the product. You want the images to stand on their own, so if that is all the shopper looked at, they can know if it was the right product for them.

Granted, some products just aren't that sexy. Some products are boring and simple. If you're selling paper clips, what do you do? You don't need to show the feeling of accomplishment buyers will get when they clip paper together. And you don't need six images of a paper clip from different perspectives (top, bottom, front, back, left, right) to really convince a potential buyer that your paper clips are the ones to buy.

Do you go with just one image? Well, you could, and it probably would convert OK—after all, the one image does effectively communicate what the product is and does. But if you do that, you're probably losing out.

Because with simple/boring products, there is a good chance the shopper has already made a decision to buy—why else would they be shopping for a boring product? What it comes down to is not whether they will buy but whose product they will choose. You don't need to use the images to convince them to buy—just to convince them to buy your product (and not the competitions' product).

You will still want to use as many images as possible to sway the shopper to choose your product. That means having a better image stack than the competition.

For an extremely boring or simple product like the paper clip example, your image stack could include the following:

- The main image of the box of paper clips on a clean white background.
- An infographic showing the dimensions of the paper clip.
- The contents of the box spilled out on a surface to visually show the quantity, possibly annotated with the exact quantity.
- The paper clip clipping some paper, maybe with an annotation of how many pages are clipped.
- A tidy desk with a big stack of neatly clipped papers.

- An infographic about your company or where the paper clips are made. What kind of steel do you use to make the paper clips?
- An infographic cross-selling your binder clips.

Even a simple example can use six (or more) images to help sell the product. More commonly, though, the bigger challenge is that it will be hard to summarize your product in just six images.

Bullet Points

Product bullet points (also known as key features) are a primary way shoppers learn about your items. After the images and the title, bullet points are probably the most important content area to fill in.

This is especially true on Amazon's desktop website, where the bullet points are displayed toward the top of the page above the fold.

Here is the listing page for Apple AirPods. The desktop shopper doesn't have to scroll far to see the bullets, which are displayed under the "About this item" heading:

Bullets on mobile are much farther down the page and are less useful to motivate shoppers. As shown here, the mobile experience is designed for the shopper to make a decision primarily on the title and images:

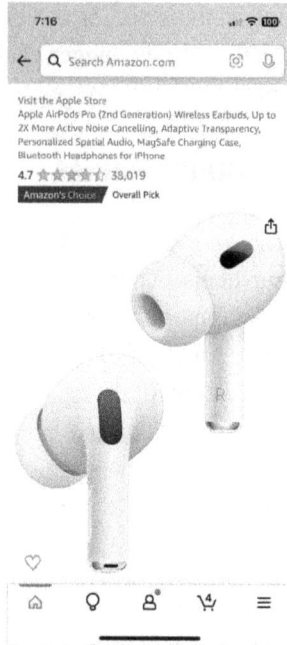

As you can see, the mobile experience is much more visual. A shopper needs to scroll past the images, past the pricing, and past the add-to-cart button to get to the bullets.

That doesn't mean bullets are not important for mobile users. They are critically important even if the shopper never sees them. The reason is that Amazon uses the bullets to understand what the product is and in which searches it should be displayed. The bullets are a key input into Amazon's search engine.

To use the tree trimmer example, Amazon on its own doesn't necessarily know that a "tree trimmer," "polesaw," and "tree pruner" are all ways to potentially describe the same product. But if you added "polesaw" and "tree pruner" in the bullets, you would give Amazon a good hint.

That way, when a shopper searches for "tree trimmer" or for "pole-saw," your product has a chance of being discovered with both searches. Bullets serve a dual purpose: to convince shoppers to buy and to provide Amazon with hints regarding the searches that shoppers may use. This brings us to our recommendations for great product bullets:

- Create five bullets for every product. Amazon requires only one but will show at least five for every product. Use all five spots.
- Bullets should be fairly short and to the point. People do not like to read paragraphs of text. A safe length is to keep your bullets around one hundred to two hundred characters each.
- Start each bullet with a benefit. A good practice is to provide the benefit in all-capital letters followed by more explanation and features.
- Incorporate key language that buyers will use to describe or search for your products. This helps Amazon figure out when to display your product and helps the shopper understand that the product is a good match.

Here are some tree trimmer examples:

- REACHES HIGHEST BRANCHES—Our telescoping tree pruner safely cuts branches over ten feet off the ground.
- FOREVER SHARP BLADE—Made of cold forged steel, it never goes dull.
- BUILT WITH SAFETY IN MIND—The blade has a protective sheath to prevent accidents.
- CONVENIENT STORAGE CASE—The polesaw folds up and stores in a compact carrying case.
- MADE IN THE USA—Proudly manufactured at our third-generation factory in Anytown, USA.

You get the idea. Follow our recommendations, and your bullets will increase conversions and help your products achieve their rightful sales.

Just like with images, it may be harder to distill the benefits and key selling points of more complex products into just five bullets. We always recommend prioritizing and focusing on the top five strongest benefits or differentiators. Thankfully, there are two additional key content areas where you can expand in more detail on your products. They are the product description and the A+ content areas.

Product Description and A+ Content

The description and A+ content areas display lower on the product page. These content areas can be used to further describe your product or brand or even your company. They are important, but not every buyer will scroll down to see them.

The first is the product description. This is a text content area up to two thousand characters long that appears somewhere around the midpoint of the product page. It can also include light formatting (paragraphs, bolded text, etc.). It is displayed more prominently on mobile than desktop. The product description is your extended opportunity to restate the benefits in the bullets, provide additional product details, and offer any other information that could help the buyer make a purchasing decision.

The A+ content area is much larger and appears either below the description or in its place. While the product description is just a space for text, A+ content can be images, text, or both.

It is extremely configurable and highly visual. It can be used to describe your product in greater detail as a virtual sell sheet or as an opportunity to reinforce your brand, speak about your company, or promote other products.

The only downside of A+ content is how far shoppers need to scroll down the page to see it. As I said, not every buyer will ever get to the A+ content before buying or abandoning your page.

The description and A+ content are particularly helpful for products that need more space to properly represent them, such as more expensive or complex products. Buyers want additional information before making a purchasing decision and are more likely to review all the content on the page.

For products that do not need additional space to describe them, we like to use the A+ content area to highlight your brand or other complementary products that you may sell.

The following is an A+ content area that spotlights their versatility. In it we've highlighted the cross-promotional functionality. This is often underused because too many manufacturers hire design-focused marketing agencies rather than agencies focused on sales and growing their Amazon business. This example does a good job of showing all the uses of A+ content. It reinforces the company branding, provides useful product information, and cross-sells the buyer.

These content areas not only help with converting shoppers into buyers but also can provide some SEO benefit to your product pages. Google and other search engines crawl this content to help understand what the Amazon page is about. Having a rich product description and A+ content not only helps inform shoppers and increases conversion but also assists Google and other search engines to send traffic to the Amazon page.

If you focus on the top three fields (title, images, and bullets) and the product description and A+ content areas, you will have created a high converting virtual salesperson to help promote your product to Amazon's millions of customers.

The next sections cover how to give shoppers more selection and how Amazon incorporates buyer feedback. Master both to ensure a bulletproof presence on Amazon.

Variations

By default, when a product is added to Amazon, it creates a unique page that is separate from all other products. This makes sense if you sell a tree trimmer. Amazon will give the tree trimmer its own unique page. But this doesn't necessarily make sense if you're selling T-shirts. By default, Amazon will create a separate page for every size and color of a T-shirt style—because each size and color is a different SKU. Instead, it makes sense to sell products like T-shirts as a member of a variation.

Variations let the shopper select a particular size, color, or style without leaving the page. For example, you would have nine distinct SKUs if you sell T-shirts in sizes small, medium, and large and in the colors red, green, and blue. But that can be just one page if you arrange those nine SKUs into a variation.

Manufacturers can set up variations, and this often improves the buyer's experience. If a buyer is looking for a specific T-shirt, they just need to search for "men's short sleeve t-shirt," click the style they like, and select the size and color from the offered variation.

Here is a variated product by Amazon with many options:

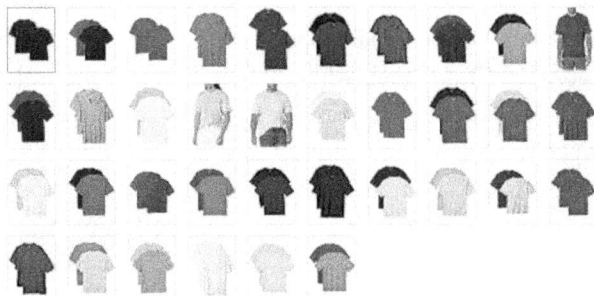

Amazon Essentials Men's Short-Sleeve Crewneck T-Shirt, Pack of 2

4.2 ★★★★☆ ∨　23,747 ratings | 95 answered questions

Price: **$7.49 - $14.**90

Free Returns on some sizes and colors ∨

prime **try before you buy**
Free 7-day try-on available for some sizes and colors.
Free shipping & returns. Learn more

Fit: As expected ∨

prime **try before you buy**

Number of Items: 2

Color: Black

Size:

| Select |
| X-Small |
| Small |
| Medium |
| Large |
| X-Large |
| XX-Large |

% Cotton; Heathers: 60% Cotton, 40% Polyester

closure

'ash

of classic regular-fit tees featuring all-cotton construction, a

As you can see, buyers can choose from thirty-six different colors and six different sizes—that's 216 combinations!

Without variations, the buyer would need to browse through all the sizes and colors in the search results and go back and forth color to color when choosing between them.

That page with 216 different SKUs takes up only one search result when a shopper types in "t-shirts."

This example outlines the trade-off with variations. If you create a variation, there is a single page where customers can choose between many options. However, that one page gets displayed as only one result on any search.

If those T-shirts were not variated, it's likely that a couple of the more popular sizes or colors would show up in people's search results instead of just one. The products get more real estate in a search but convert less well because the shopper must select the right size and color before they buy.

Variating is a trade-off. Products with lower sales typically benefit from being grouped, if possible, while products with higher sales may benefit from less variations. Deciding which strategy will drive more sales for your products depends on your product specifics, the standard searches your buyers make, and your typical search rankings on those searches.

This concludes our coverage of some of the product page attributes that you can control to maximize your conversion. What we discussed are just the top ones; there are dozens more as well as many category-specific fields. Providing Amazon with as much information as you can about your products is best, though use the recommendations in this book to help prioritize your efforts.

The last section covers major product page sections that can make or break your products . . . but you cannot control it directly.

Reviews, Ratings, and Q&A

Reviews and ratings and the Q&A sections are created by Amazon buyers. They are all designed to use buyers' experiences with your products to help guide future shoppers.

Reviews are written primarily from verified buyers of your product. They can include images and even videos. They are located below the main product section, and Amazon attempts to highlight both positive and negative reviews.

Ratings use a one- to five-star feedback system. Verified buyers can provide an overall rating as well as category-specific ratings such as "sturdiness" or "fit." The weighted average of all the ratings is displayed next to the product everywhere on the site.

You want a lot of reviews and the average of the reviews to be good (4+). Products with more than twenty reviews perform better in advertising, products with a lot of reviews (more than one hundred) convert better overall, and products with higher review ratings will beat products with lower review ratings.

The key to getting good reviews and ratings is having a page that accurately describes your product and offers it at a good price. Buyers need to know what to expect, and the product must deliver the "promise" at a competitive price.

Customers give negative reviews if their expectations are not met or if they feel they got a bad value. Accurately describing your product and pricing it competitively will eliminate most bad reviews.

Occasional bad reviews are not actually bad. Shoppers are not expecting a perfect product. Bad reviews help shoppers know the limitations of your product. You just don't want bad reviews to be too frequent. That could be a sign of a quality issue or a missed expectation.

Questions and answers are submitted by potential buyers. The Q&A section is located immediately below the core product section. Amazon allows manufacturers, sellers, and even customers who purchased the item to answer questions. As a manufacturer, it is critical for you to actively participate in this section on Amazon.

As you grow, you want to establish a process to quickly answer customer questions. Questions are a sign that the listing page is missing important information or is unclear. For every shopper who has a question and asks it, there could be dozens who have the same question and don't. Answering their questions makes your listing page more effective at converting future shoppers.

All these are critical areas of customer feedback and help future customers make purchasing decisions. They can be important resources for your company as well, for three reasons.

First, buyers trust the reviews and ratings. All things being equal, Amazon shoppers will buy the product with more reviews and higher ratings.

This results in an advantage for the incumbent products. The longer you've been on the platform, the more reviews you naturally get. They make your product pages a long-term asset to your company.

As the saying goes, the best time to get your products on Amazon was five years ago, and the second best time is today. Ensuring that your products are on Amazon and are represented properly is critical to maintaining a high feedback rating.

Second, reviews give you, the manufacturer, valuable product feedback. Learn what people love and hate about your products—and your competitors' products. Use that information to improve how you sell the product or even to make a new, improved product.

In chapter 2, I shared the story of the oil pan being used as a tray under college dorm fridges. We learned about that from reading the product reviews. And from those insights, we adjusted the marketing to better position the product for that usage.

The Amazon questions section is another great source for insights. It's hard to anticipate every question a buyer might have, but with the Q&A section, you don't have to. Potential buyers can ask questions, and you, as the manufacturer, as well as other buyers, can answer them. For every person who asks a question, there are probably hundreds who had the same question but didn't ask. Not only can they get the answer immediately but also, if it makes sense, you can add the answer to the bullets and other parts of the product page.

Third, reviews give you an early-warning signal of issues. Amazon customers are quick to leave negative feedback. Although this is frustrating, one benefit is that if you have a quality issue, you will learn about it on Amazon ahead of almost any other channel.

One of our clients sold a product with a lid. We kept seeing reviews complaining of leaks. It turned out there was a defect in the design, but none of the manufacturer's other channels brought it up. The manufacturer modified the product to eliminate the issue because they got a quality warning from customer reviews.

I've covered a lot of ground here, but this section is not exhaustive. There is a lot more nuance and content available that we haven't even discussed.

However, if you focus on these areas in the way that I just described, your product pages will easily be in the top 10 percent of all product pages on Amazon.

Once you have a virtual salesperson, the next step is to arm them with a deal that buyers can't refuse—using promotions.

Promotions

Amazon has several different promotional opportunities. We'll go into some of the biggest, but the general purpose of promotions is to increase sales by giving buyers a deal.

Promotions are usually temporary but should have two effects. First, the promotion should increase sales during the promotional period. If you offer 20 percent off "this week only," you should get more sales this week compared to a normal week.

The second, and often equally important goal of promotions, is to create an ongoing lift in sales. After the promotion expires, the increase in sales will result in relatively higher rankings in search results. This often brings about more sales.

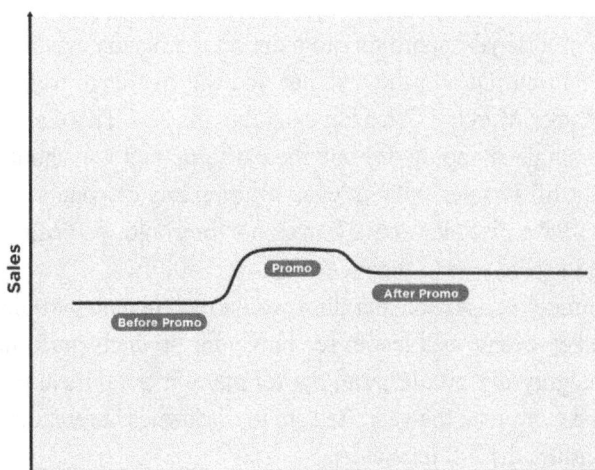

Sales spike during a promotion and hopefully normalize at a higher level after a promotion.

The benefit of the promotion is not only the increase in sales during the promo but also any lift in sales after the promotion. Whether the lift happens and how great it is depends on the competitive landscape. Promotions technically also increase traffic to your pages—potentially by a lot. Amazon gives a ton of visibility to promotions because buyers love them. You can easily drive two to three times the typical traffic to a page with effective use of a promotion. Putting that on top with a much higher conversion rate can drive a ton of sales.

In some very competitive markets, promotions are more the norm than the exception. When a customer is shopping, the vast majority of products will have coupons or other deals on them. In those markets, you are at a competitive disadvantage if you don't promote. If you are in a market like this, promotions are more a cost of doing business. In those cases, you don't really promote to see a lift but instead to remain competitive and to ensure a reasonable conversion.

Amazon has many different promotional opportunities. The following are some of the more popular options for you to consider.

Events

The first promotional opportunity to mention is Amazon events. The two biggest are Prime Day in the summer and the five days from Thanksgiving to Cyber Monday (Amazon calls this the T5). These are some of the busiest single shopping days on the platform, and you should expect a significant lift in sales without even offering any discounts. However, if you do offer a discount above Amazon's threshold, you can officially participate in these events and receive extra visibility.

Assuming you have the margin, I would recommend participating in one of the key events as a test to see how your products perform. Every product category is a bit different, but for many it is a critical promotion that can make or break the year. Be sure to track sales before, during, and after to measure the full impact.

Coupons

The second promotional opportunity is couponing. Amazon coupons work just like traditional coupons—you offer customers a percentage or dollar amount off. Amazon highlights products with coupons in search results, which yield higher click-through rates:

Sponsored ⓘ	WGCC **Meal Prep Containers**, 50	Ben
Meal Prep Containers, [34oz 50Pack] Food **Prep Containers** with Lids, Disposable To Go **Containers**, Plastic Food Storage **Containers** with Lids,...	Pack Extra-thick Food Storage **Containers** with Lids, Disposable Bento Box Reusable Plastic Bento...	**Con** with Dur:
★★★★☆ ⌄ 258 100+ bought in past month	★★★★☆ ⌄ 5,655 6K+ bought in past month	★★ 1K+
$19⁹⁹ ($0.40/Count)	**$23**⁹⁹ List: $27.99	$1·
Save $3.00 with coupon	Save 5% with coupon	FREE
FREE delivery **Sat, Aug 19** on $25 of items shipped by Amazon	FREE delivery **Sat, Aug 19** on $25 of items shipped by Amazon	ship Or fa
Or fastest delivery **Wed, Aug 16**	Or fastest delivery **Tomorrow, Aug 15**	
	More Buying Choices $21.49 (2 used & new offers)	

One product offers $3.00 off and the other 5 percent off—if you clip the coupon on the product page before checking out.

Coupons increase traffic to your listings because it is advertised as pictured in the search results. This increase in interested traffic on its own boosts sales. Once on the page, buyers need to clip the coupon on the listing page to get the promotion. This again increases sales through a growth in conversion. Coupons increase sales two ways—by boosting traffic and by growing conversion.

The funny thing is that not everyone remembers to clip the coupon. Some shoppers are so used to just adding an item to their cart that they forget that extra step. If you offer $3.00 off, it may cost you only $2.50 on average due to people forgetting to clip the coupon. Between the traffic increase and the discount due to clipping, this can be an extremely effective method of promotion.

Subscribe and Save

Many products are consumable—shoppers will buy them again and again. Amazon's Subscribe and Save program lets buyers sign up for periodic delivery. Customers can receive the product on subscription every two months, for example.

Subscribe & Save:
5% | 10%
$42.83

Save 5% now and up to 10% on repeat deliveries.
• No fees
• Cancel anytime
Learn more
Get it Saturday, Aug 19

In Stock

Qty: 1 ∨

Deliver every:

1 month (Most common) ∨

Set Up Now

Ships from and sold by Amazon.com

Instead of selling the product once and having to compete for the next sale, you get the repeat purchase for free if the buyer subscribes.

Amazon will turn this on for your listings automatically if they detect repeat purchases, and you can create promotional offers to incentivize buyers to select Subscribe and Save over a single purchase.

These promotions can have a huge payoff, as Subscribe and Save buyers typically end up purchasing the same product multiple times. As an example, let's say your product sells for $50 and your profit is $10. If you spend your entire profit—$10—on a Subscribe and Save promotion, you break even if the customer buys your product twice. Every purchase after the second is incremental profit due to the program. Some buyers will repeat purchases a dozen or more times, so the ROI can be huge.

Subscribe and Save is an example of an program where it makes sense to understand the lifetime value (LTV) of an Amazon customer. For some consumable products, getting the repeat business can dramatically increase the LTV. The higher the LTV, the more you can spend to acquire new customers. What might not make sense to pay to acquire a single sale may make a great deal of sense to pay to acquire a customer who makes multiple purchases.

Business Promotions

The final opportunity I'll mention is business-focused promotions. I've touched on this before, but it's worth going into a bit more detail here. Amazon Business is a special program for business buyers that offers them exclusive discounts and business-focused buying tools. Businesses can create Amazon Business buying accounts, which receive access to business-only pricing that is not available to regular Amazon users.

Amazon has a variety of promotions that you can implement to attract their business buyers. Many of our B2B clients are extremely excited about this, as most of their sales in other channels are to businesses. However, Amazon Business is relatively small compared to Amazon overall. There are likely more businesses buying on Amazon outside of Amazon Business than through the program. Although business promotions are great, it's important that you don't rely on them exclusively to attract business customers. Ideally, you design your catalog and your offers so that they appeal to businesses regardless of whether they participate in Amazon Business.

This example shows grease being sold on Amazon. It's available in 14-oz. cartridges, which are for single use. The target would be weekend mechanics and hobbyists and for casual residential use.

The manufacturer also sells a 400-lb. drum of the same product, which is obviously for a very different market. The great thing about Amazon is that you can target both the hobbyist and the professional segments from the same page using different offers in a variation.

These recommendations will make your pages some of the most extremely converting pages on Amazon—shoppers will quickly convert to buyers. You are now ready to focus on the next step—acquiring eyeballs to view and buy your products. The formula for Amazon riches is very simple: send massive amounts of traffic to pages that convert like crazy!

CHAPTER 9

HOW TO FLOOD YOUR AMAZON PAGES WITH QUALIFIED TRAFFIC

In the last chapter, we shared how to create your virtual salesperson so that your pages convert. But the best converting page in the world doesn't drive sales if buyers don't find it.

In this chapter, we discuss exactly what you need to do to flood your pages with massive amounts of qualified shoppers.

As a reminder, Sales = Conversion × Traffic.

SALES = TRAFFIC x CONVERSION

Traffic Drivers
- Organic search results
- Pay Per Click ads
- Promotions
- External Traffic
- Selection
- Branding

Everything you do to increase page conversion or traffic to your pages boosts your sales. But you need both to win—great converting pages alone is not enough. That's why having these strategies to drive traffic to your pages is so important.

Types of Traffic

There are two types of traffic you can send to your products on Amazon—paid and organic. Paid traffic is when you pay Amazon to advertise your products and drive shoppers to your product pages. Organic traffic comes when a shopper conducts a search and then clicks on your product in a search result slot that your product earned from its sales history.

Here is a portion of the search results for "hammers":

The first four results in row one are sponsored results. This means that they are paid advertisements. The last product in the first row and the first three products in the second row are organic, natural results. This means that they have earned those spots from their sales history.

Organic traffic is driven by Amazon's search engine algorithm that picks the best products to display for a given search. You want your products to display as high on the page as possible for the most relevant search terms. Shoppers generally click on products at the top of a search result page more often.

Amazon determines your product's organic search rank (position on the search results page) based on its sales history and relevance to the search term. The products that display on the top of a page in the organic results have a proven history of converting well for search.

Unproven or new products will be displayed much lower in organic search results and likely on a secondary page. If there are a lot of products, it may be impossible to find a new product organically at all. Virtually all sales for a search occur on the first page of search results. If your product is not on the first page of a search result, it is likely not getting any organic traffic from customers for that particular search.

Organic traffic is great for proven winners. Amazon gives them top billing, which in turn drives a ton of traffic, which in turn drives a ton of sales. This virtuous cycle drives the sustained sales and growth of established bestsellers. But this is bad news if you're not already an established winner.

Paid traffic is the answer for products that do not organically rank on key search terms. Paid traffic (a.k.a. advertising) lets you buy your way to the front of a search result. This not only will get you relevant traffic and sales immediately but also teaches Amazon what relevant searches drive conversion on your products. Amazon will then use this knowledge to build your organic rank, which means you'll get sales from organic traffic over time as well.

The optimal Amazon traffic strategy combines these two sources of traffic in a way that maximizes performance over the long term. Your products likely will not organically rank for the most competitive and lucrative searches at first. Ranking for top search terms can take months or even years to build up enough sales history. To do that, you use advertising to "buy" placement to those search result pages. This may be expensive, but over time the cost of advertising relative to your sales will go down as your organic sales increase.

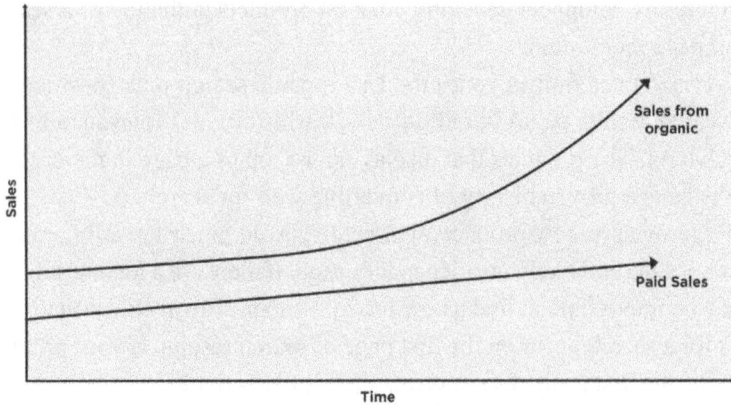

This graph illustrates how traffic and sales grow over time. At first it's hard to get significant organic (free) traffic. You need advertising to bring initial visibility to your products. This builds a sales history that allows Amazon to start driving organic traffic to the page. With two sources of traffic, sales increase faster. This causes your products to rank even higher, which in turn brings even more organic traffic. After a while, paid traffic is relatively small compared to the overall sales.

This is why building a listing page and hoping buyers will come is a bad strategy. Creating a great page does not guarantee you the traffic you deserve. In fact, if all you do is create a page, you can be assured that you will *not* get the traffic you deserve. You need to make that happen.

It takes a significant amount of sales for a product to appear on a competitive search results page. If you don't speed up the process with advertising, it could take years—if ever—for your product to develop a proven sales history on its own.

The next two sections detail exactly how to best create paid and organic traffic. We cover paid first, because it's often what is required to kick-start a virtuous cycle of sales for your products.

Paid Traffic: Amazon Advertising

Paid traffic not only directly increases the traffic that a listing receives but also causes the listing to appear higher in search results. Traffic generated from advertising is the primary impact and is great. But the virtuous cycle kicks in when the sales from that traffic drive higher search result ranks.

This can be illustrated by one of our clients who launched a kitchen appliance and used this strategy to drive traffic to their new product. In the first month, they spent $17,000 advertising the product and drove only $19,000 in sales. If you look just at that month, they lost a ton of money—they spent almost 100 percent of their revenue advertising the product. You could say they essentially gave the product away.

But they knew that launching a product was an investment in creating sales momentum and wanted to build some organic rank. They were in a highly competitive category and knew their investment would pay off.

They persisted, and they continued to spend a significant portion of their sales in advertising.

By the sixth month, it was a completely different story. The majority of their traffic and sales came organically. The product surpassed $150,000 per month (basically ten times month one), and advertising was only 10 percent of sales, which was well within their budget.

Our client knew the market potential of their product and the value of creating a bestseller. They were able to take a longer perspective to calculate ROI, and it paid off big-time.

All of Amazon's advertising occurs on a platform called Amazon Ads. It used to be called Amazon Marketing Services (AMS), and it stands as a separate website from both the vendor and the seller portals. Amazon Ads is a complex and evolving application, and it would be easy to write a whole book on it. And the day the book is released, it would be out of date. For our purposes, I'll introduce some key and (hopefully) timeless points about advertising on Amazon.

Advertising Isn't Optional

Here is the first key point: Advertising on Amazon is not optional. It's a huge profit center for Amazon, so it's fully integrated into their platform, and they give advertised products extremely prominent placement on virtually all pages. Products that advertise leverage this placement and reach more customers. As a result, they steal traffic from established competition. If you don't advertise, it will be much harder to gain momentum on new products, and good-selling products will bleed sales to more aggressive advertising competitors.

After all, it's in Amazon's best interests to give traffic to manufacturers that will pay the most for that traffic. From Amazon's perspective, they make money on the sale as well as on any advertising the buyer clicks on to make the purchase. So it's a win-win for Amazon. As a manufacturer, this may be a bitter pill to swallow, as you have to pay Amazon handsomely for the traffic that you probably should get anyway. However, the sooner you accept this reality—even if you don't like it—the faster you can leverage that reality to your advantage.

Strategically, paid traffic not only builds your organic traffic but also protects it from the competition. There is both an offensive and a defensive aspect to advertising.

Advertising lets you break into new search result territory—that's offensive advertising. But what you can do, so can your competition. That's why it's important to keep advertising defensively even after you've achieved your ranking goals. Defensive advertising makes it more expensive (and many times unaffordable) for new entrants to steal the success you built.

This probably sounds costly. After all, I'm telling you to spend money advertising new products before you get sales and then to continue spending even after you accomplish your sales goals. Although it is true that advertising is an additional cost, the good news is that you have complete control over the expense and don't necessarily have to spend a fortune.

Advertising Gives You Immediate Results

This takes us to the second key point—advertising is pay as you go with near real-time results.

Amazon Ads does not require long-term contracts, and you can evaluate the impact almost in real time.

In most cases, you pay when a site visitor clicks on an ad and views one of your pages. Amazon then tracks whether the visitor buys your product, giving you the results to compute the ROI of the advertising campaign.

The spend accrues throughout the day against daily budgets and also against monthly budgets. Spending can be stopped, increased, or changed at any time.

This immediate feedback allows advertisers to optimize their advertising for the goals they have. In most cases, you want to optimize your advertising for ROI on ad spend—get the most sales for a given amount spent on advertising.

The metrics they provide allow you to spend more where it's working and less where it's not. And because you know the amount of sales your advertising is generating, you can determine the ROI of advertising on a unit basis and with your Amazon business overall. This feature makes it an extremely powerful tool in building your Amazon business.

Amazon reports advertising performance in terms of ROAS and ACoS. ROAS is return on advertising spend and is the retail sales generated/spent on advertising. ACoS is advertising cost of sales and is spent on advertising/retail sales generated.

The terms are basically interchangeable in that they are directly related:

$$ROAS = 1 / ACoS$$

We have clients with ACoS targets of 4 percent (ROAS target of 25) and clients with ACoS targets of 40 percent (ROAS target of 2.5). The targets for ROAS and ACoS depend on several factors—your product margins, the competitiveness of your product category, your product's life cycle, and your business goals.

Here's how ROAS is related to these important factors:

- *Margins:* If you spend 100 percent of your profit margin, your ACoS = profit margin. This would be the break-even point on the advertised sale. If your ACoS is < profit margin, you are making money on every advertised (and unadvertised) sale. If your ACoS is > profit margin, you are losing money on advertised sales but may still be making profit overall. You would only want ROAS > profit margin if you are aggressively trying to improve the search results performance of a product.

- *Competition:* How much you pay for advertising depends on the competitiveness of the niche in which you're advertising. Advertising is a competitive auction process, so you bid on advertising placements, and the bidder who is most likely to generate advertising revenue for Amazon wins. Markets with a lot of advertising competition pay more for clicks, on average, than markets with less competition.

- *Product life cycle:* Generally, it makes sense to advertise more when launching a product or with products with limited sales history. When Amazon doesn't know much about your product (due to lack of history), they don't know what traffic, if any, will convert into sales. In this case, the right strategy is to use advertising to incentivize Amazon to send traffic to an unproven product. The paid traffic will generate the first sales and give Amazon critical data on the types of searches and customers who turn into converting buyers. This is why you will spend more on advertising on a relative basis early in a product's life cycle.

- *Your business goals:* The amount you will spend on advertising depends on your business goals and overall temperament.

Theoretically, advertising pays for itself as long as it generates more profit than it costs. That point of diminishing returns can result in an incredibly large advertising budget due to Amazon's size.

Although we have some clients who attempt to maximize the absolute return and regularly spend upward of 25 percent or more of their revenue on advertising, most are not that aggressive. It's critical to set advertising targets that are not only profitable but also fit into your larger business priorities.

Advertising Requires Goals

This gets us to the third point on advertising: you must set clear goals and then track results against them.

Two common ways to specify advertising goals are in terms of ROI and absolute spend. We prefer ROI-based goals, as they maximize growth. After all, if you can make two dollars for every one dollar you spend, why cap that with a monthly budget?

However, not every company can operate with that flexibility. Because of this, most accounts we work with have both ROI targets and maximum monthly budgets.

ROI targets should be defined at the product level based on the factors mentioned previously and in terms of ROAS or ACoS. In addition to those metrics, we also recommend tracking the total advertising cost of sales (TACoS), which is the total advertising spend / total sales.

Remember this graph from earlier in the chapter that shows how traffic changes over time?

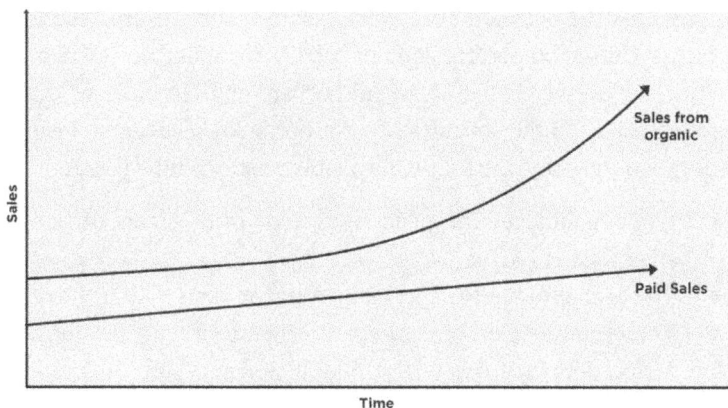

While that is happening, here is what happens to the key advertising metrics:

- Your ACoS will likely start higher than your target. But as you optimize your advertising, your ACoS will reach your target ACoS. This process could take a couple of months.
- Your ROAS, the inverse of ACoS, will start low and increase.
- Your TACoS will start high, as most sales initially are from advertising. Generally, this should decrease over time. Often the TACoS is used to set next year's advertising budget.

As a reminder, all this happens because of the virtuous cycles.

- As you and Amazon gain more information about what searches and customers convert into sales, the sales generated by advertising increase.
- This also causes your products to appear higher and higher in search results for searches that convert.
- This causes you to get more organic traffic, which results in increased sales over time.
- This is why even if you spend more and more on advertising, your TACoS—the total cost of advertising as a percentage of entire sales—can continue to decrease over time.

This is how traffic and key advertising metrics *should* perform. However, this begs the question as to what exactly good performance looks like. Is an ACoS of 10 percent good or bad? What about an ROAS of 5?

The short answer is that there are no hard-and-fast rules of thumb. It really depends on the specifics of your products, niche, and business. However, we can share the following average metrics for Amazon:

- Large manufacturers spend an average of 6 percent of sales on advertising (TACoS).
- The average advertising click on Amazon costs (CPC) one dollar.
- The average ACoS on Amazon is 30 percent for sellers and less for vendors (approximately 15 to 20 percent)

These are accurate as of summer 2023, but take them with a grain of salt. The average metric includes entire categories of products with financials that are massively different from your products. The only way you can proceed with advertising is to start with a bottoms up analysis of what your goals are and then a series of controlled advertising experiments to see if your goals are realistic and can be achieved.

You can do this only by spending an initial amount to learn how the market and the specific advertising tactics you implement perform. You can then learn and adjust accordingly.

As we said before, the only wrong answer is spending zero.

The only rule of thumb we can provide you without doing a deeper analysis on your specifics is that you should be spending at least a few thousand dollars a month on advertising. This is likely justified on an ROI basis even on the smallest accounts. Spending a few thousand a month should give you enough results to measure and to know what your true budget should be.

Organic Traffic: The Key to Sustainable Long-Term Success

Advertising is great in that it allows you to jump-start sales on quality products immediately. It's the price of admission, gets you your first sales, and allows you to scale up. But you pay for it. To go from one thousand paid visitors to ten thousand, you will pay ten times (or more).

Paying for your traffic (and sales) isn't necessarily bad business. It really depends on your margins and how much you pay. But what makes you the real money on Amazon is usually not the paid traffic but the organic traffic—free traffic that Amazon automatically sends to your products for having a proven right to win.

As a reminder, when a shopper searches on Amazon, Amazon tries to connect them with the best matching products—that is, the products most likely to convert based on the shopper's searches, profile, and other behavior.

Amazon reserves a portion of the search results for advertised products, where Amazon makes money if the shopper just clicks the product. But most of the page is usually devoted to organic results—that is, Amazon's unbiased best guess as to what the shopper is looking for.

Getting into the organic results is critical. The magic starts to happen when your product enters the top organic results for key search terms. For any given search, 80 percent of traffic and sales go to results on the first page. And a majority of that goes to the top three results. The sales difference between a product in the top three versus the bottom of the page can easily be ten times or more in some niches.

You want all your products to be a top result for their primary keyword. That's how you turn them into bestsellers.

An added benefit is that once you are a top result for a search term, you also pay less to advertise and keep your products there. The cost to advertise depends on how much you pay as well as on how effectively your product converts. Bestselling products pay less than unproven products.

Not only is there a virtuous cycle where paid traffic increases organic traffic but also there is a virtuous cycle between the listing optimization you do to create your virtual salesperson and the traffic you get.

As you optimize your content, your products will become relevant for new searches. Paid advertising will get them placed there initially, but over time they will gain a higher organic search rank. This will drive more organic traffic, which increases sales. Content updates and the increased sales make your products eligible for new searches and markets. Continuous improvement and the powers of Amazon create a virtuous cycle that directly drives sales!

This begs two key questions: What are the top search terms for your products? And once you know them, how do you make your product become a top result for those search terms? Read the next two sections to become a pro.

How to Find Your Top Moneymaking Search Terms

Search terms are what people type in on Amazon when looking for a product. The problem is that there can be dozens of popular search terms for any given product. The reason is that many products have multiple names, descriptions, and uses, all of which can be incorporated as a potential search term that a buyer enters. Accounting for that and misspellings (and Spanish), there are probably hundreds of different search terms that are relevant for any one of your products.

How do you find your top moneymaking search terms? The answer is that you don't! Amazon does the hard work for you. All you have to do is give Amazon some hints. Those hints are called keywords, and they help Amazon match your products to the searches your buyers make.

The next section gives an example of how Amazon's search engine works. This will help you understand how keywords relate to search terms. Knowing that makes it much easier to find top moneymaking search terms.

Amazon Search Secrets Revealed

Amazon search is the primary mechanism by which shoppers find products. Visitors type in search terms, and Amazon displays the most relevant results. As we discussed, one key factor, relevancy, is based on historical sales. If people entering a specific search buy your product, Amazon knows your product is highly relevant for that search.

But this doesn't explain how Amazon would associate your product with a particular search term in the first place. That's where the keywords—the hints—come in. Amazon considers every word and phrase in your title, bullets, and select other fields on your listings to be keywords for your product. If the words people are searching for appear in your title or in one of the other key fields, Amazon knows the product is potentially relevant to the search.

Let's look at an example. Say you sell a USB charger that plugs into a wall outlet. A top keyword for this might be "usb charger." Amazon would match this phrase against user searches. Amazon does this by matching word for word, so the keyword phrase "usb charger" would match searches such as these:

- usb charger
- usb charger block
- usb wall charger
- iphone charger usb
- usb plug in wall charger
- anker usb charger
- 65 watt usb c charger
- double usb wall charger
- usb a charger
- usb fast charger
- dual usb charger
- dual usb wall charger
- wall charger with usb ports
- usb chargers
- usb a charger block
- usb phone charger
- usb wall charger fast charging
- usb box wall charger

The phrase "usb charger" would even match the single words "usb" and "charger" based on how Amazon's search engine works, along with every other search term that contains "usb" and "charger." The "usb charger" keyword covers a lot of ground—there are thousands of searches that match those keywords. But that doesn't mean your product will rank equally for all. Amazon takes into account your sales history and specifically what other people searched for when they bought your product (as well as many other factors) to ultimately determine how prominently to display your product.

In our example, let's assume that your USB charger is not a fast charger. Then it will convert better for "dual usb wall charger" searches than for "usb wall charger fast charging." Amazon will start to rank your product higher for better converting searches. In this case, your product will rank higher for "dual usb wall charger" and maybe not at all for "usb wall charger fast charging" and other "fast charging" searches.

To summarize, your product listing consists of product keywords. Amazon uses these keywords (and other factors) to determine whether a particular shopper's search is relevant. The best way to help ensure relevance is to choose keywords that contain the same words and phrases that potential buyers would use in searches.

That is how Amazon's search works in a nutshell. Now that we know those basics, let's figure out how to pick keywords that will get the most buyer searches.

What Are My Product's Keywords?

As we just covered, having the right words in your product title and bullets is important—it's a critical signal that Amazon uses to connect your product to potential buyers.

Logically, this makes sense. You should call your product what your potential buyers call it. A British wrench manufacturer will sell a lot more products on US Amazon.com if they call their product a wrench and not a spanner, which is the British English word for wrench.

The first way you can determine your keywords is simply by using your market knowledge and experience. Many products have simple and obvious keywords that people would use to refer to them in an everyday situation.

This is a good place to start. Like with many things on Amazon, it's more important to take action than to delay and overanalyze. Doing this gives you results that you can use to learn and adjust. The market's response (i.e., sales or no sales) will tell you if you got it right. After all, the answer to the question "What are my product's keywords?" is "Whatever the market says they are."

You can often quickly validate whether you have good keywords by using them in an Amazon search. Amazon will show you the products they think are the most relevant. Get what you expect? Then you're probably on the right track.

A second way to determine potential keywords is by looking at established competition. There is a good chance that the bestsellers in your niche are using the right words in their titles and bullets. You can also use tools such as Helium 10 and Amazon Brand Analytics to get actual searches that your competitors rank and convert for.

Assuming that the same keywords are relevant for your product, this strategy can give you immediate market validation for keywords that likely work. This is a great tactic if you're just starting out. An additional benefit of doing this rather than just guessing is that you might discover keywords you didn't expect.

And when you're in a marathon and far behind, it's worth looking at what the person in the lead is doing. Once you're neck and neck, that's when you can start breaking your own ground with the third and fourth tactics.

A third source is to use Amazon Ads. Advertising will provide you with details on exactly what searches convert for your product and their relative performance. (This assumes that you are advertising your products, and if you read the previous sections, you should be!) This data is very similar to what Amazon uses to determine your product relevancy for searches, so it's a valuable source of information.

A fourth source is looking at product feedback. If your product has a lot of reviews and questions, you'll likely find words and phrases that buyers are using that describe your product in ways you haven't thought of. We always recommend reviewing feedback and incorporating those insights into the product listings. This includes words and phrases that buyers use that could be valuable keywords.

The goal is to identify a handful, at most, of keywords that capture the vast majority of searches people enter for your products. How do you know if you have the right keywords?

- Your rank on keyword searches should improve. If "usb charger" is your number one keyword for your product, over time your rank for that search should increase. Amazon rewards the right keywords, and you can see that in improved rank in search results.
- Advertising related to the keyword should perform well. It should convert well and drive a significant amount of advertised sales for the product.

Now that you know how to find the right keywords, let's talk about turning that knowledge into sales.

How to Rank Higher and Get More Sales Than Your Competition

The words "usb charger" get around thirty thousand searches a month. Searches that contain "usb charger" easily get around another thirty to sixty thousand searches a month.

If you follow the steps in the previous section, you'll quickly learn that related terms such as "iphone charger" and "portable charger" get over five hundred thousand searches each.

It's tempting to focus on the biggest and most popular searches. Because search popularity is a rough approximation for market size, you can infer that the iPhone charger market is ten to twenty times the size of the USB charger market, so it might make sense to position your product for the much larger market.

But that logic is wrong, as it doesn't leverage how Amazon actually works. Amazon operates as a flywheel (see chapter 3), and that process rewards products that sell. The virtuous cycle means that if a product sells well, then Amazon knows it has great market fit and promotes it (which causes it to sell more). New and unproven products don't have that sales history and because of that are unproven in Amazon's eyes.

That is why the winning strategy is to start small, get small successes, and grow over time. Become the number one bestseller in the smallest niche possible and then use that success to become a bestseller in a slightly broader niche. Build on existing successes to create larger successes. Grow the product over time into bigger and bigger niches.

If you're launching a USB charger, it's much easier and cheaper to become the bestselling "wall charger with usb ports" product first than to try to directly get traction in the "usb charger" market.

"Wall charger with usb ports" is more of a niche, specialized search term than "usb charger." There are fewer products that are a good fit, and your product has fewer competitors to beat. Additionally, because it's so specific, this search term becomes highly relevant to your product. Shoppers typing in "wall charger with usb ports" end up buying "wall chargers with usb ports" at a much higher rate than shoppers typing in "usb charger." Not only is the market smaller (and more winnable) but also your product would have the highest right to win for this specialized search.

Winning the smaller market is just a stepping stone. The success in "wall charger with usb ports" will have halo effects in related larger markets. Over time, your rank in "usb charger" will increase naturally, even if you're just targeting "wall charger with usb ports." At a certain point, your product becomes competitive in the larger market, and you can then shift your focus to conquer a bigger market at that time.

Rinse and repeat as necessary. You keep winning and moving into bigger and bigger markets. You do this until you surpass your competition and become the number one selling product for all relevant keywords in your market.

This is a common strategy we implement with our clients. Often the first market they dominate is searches for their brand name. It's smaller than the market overall, and they have an extreme right to win. If your business name is Acme and you sell widgets, you'll be the natural number one choice for "acme widgets" searches.

Once you dominate your branded searches, you can expand to unbranded searches. As we illustrated in the USB charger example, you want to start with more specific unbranded keywords first and then eventually broaden and expand as you build success.

Previously we recommended "wrench" as a better, more logical keyword than "spanner" if you're selling wrenches in the US market. Although this is true, it doesn't take into account the keyword targeting progression that may make the most sense. Royal Industries, a British tool manufacturer, may have more luck winning with the "spanner" keyword when starting. Their US fan base may be small, but it's probably searching for their products using the British English word "spanner." As they dominate that niche market, they can then expand their target keyword focus to a broader "wrenches."

As they move to larger and larger markets, that doesn't mean Royal Industries abandons the markets they historically dominated. They'll want to retain the success they've already achieved. If they first won in the "spanner" market, it may make sense to continue to target that keyword even as they go on to win in the larger "wrench" market.

Here is a row of top-selling wrenches:

These are the first four organic results for the search "wrench."

Notice how the third one has the keyword "spanner" in its title? This is an example of keeping one foot in the smaller "spanner" niche while primarily targeting the larger "wrench" market. That Edward Tools wrench is the number two organic result for "spanner" and the number three organic result for "wrench." Impressive.

This example illustrates the exact process to apply to your products. The primary keyword you're targeting today should be incorporated into the product title toward the front. Secondary keywords or benefits can be added to your title after that.

Any other keywords you want to target, as well as all the great benefits of your product, can be added to the product bullets. We covered the basics of titles and bullets in chapter 8, but it's worth noting here specifically how to incorporate primary and secondary keywords.

The basic title structure will look like this: [Brand Name] [primary keyword], [secondary keyword and/or benefit, key feature, etc.].

The basic bullet structure will lead with benefits, have key features/ differentiators, and use secondary keywords throughout the text. If you have keywords that don't naturally fit into either the title or the bullets, you can add them to the backend in the generic keywords field.

Amazon provides the generic keywords field as a place to put keywords that will help Amazon identify searches for the product using terms that do not make sense to have in the main listing visible to buyers. This would be a good place to put the Spanish-language translation of your top keywords. If you're selling wrenches, you might add "llave inglesa" in the generic keywords, since it wouldn't make sense to have Spanish in the title or in the bullets.

Adding the correct primary keyword into your title and bullets alone doesn't guarantee success. You need to couple this with paid advertising that also targets the same keywords. This can be done with manual ads that specifically target the keywords or with autotargeting campaigns that will automatically pull keywords out of your titles and bullets. This advertising jump-starts sales and creates the signals Amazon needs to know that the keyword is relevant. Amazon increases your rank for a keyword the more signals of relevancy they get.

You know this works if the following happens:

- Your products start ranking higher on the page for your keyword. You can monitor this manually, or there are many tools that will do this for you.
- TACoS (total advertising cost of sales) goes down.

And, of course, sales go up. This is the primary and most visible metric. Because of Amazon's winner-takes-most market, the product that dominates the right keyword often takes the majority of sales. You will know you're winning when your sales growth explodes!

The previous chapter shared how to make your Amazon virtual salesperson sell your products. Follow that guidance, and when shoppers visit your pages, they'll convert into buyers better than 90 percent of the other products on Amazon.

This chapter covered the basics on traffic—how Amazon decides who gets traffic and how to get the traffic you need to your high converting pages. Traffic is a winner-takes-most game. If you do it right, it will flood your product pages with shoppers driving massive sales growth.

Now that you have this knowledge, the next couple of chapters will help you operationalize it and turn Amazon into one of your top-performing customers!

CHAPTER 10

HOW TO SYSTEMATIZE AND DELEGATE SO THAT YOUR AMAZON BUSINESS RUNS ITSELF

A mazon is made for manufacturers. I've seen how Bezos's baby grows new business, improves operations, and brings manufacturers closer to their end customers. And after reading this far into the book, I hope you agree.

My clients view Amazon as a vital part of their business. For most, it's their fastest-growing customer, and for many, Amazon has become a top five customer.

But as much as I like Amazon and believe it's a huge positive for manufacturers, I cannot deny one ugly truth: Amazon is not easy to work with. They are more difficult than traditional customers—Walmart, Target, Home Depot, and pretty much any other large retailer or e-commerce company.

In fact, almost universally, clients admit that Amazon is one of the most difficult customers they have. But there is a big difference between a difficult and demanding customer that you are happy to have and a painful customer that you hate and who is so difficult that they make you want to rip your hair out. This chapter will help ensure that Amazon stays in the first category and does not make the leap into the second.

The key is to engage with Amazon with your eyes open and aware of the critical needs. Amazon will have multiple touch points within your company, and key roles must be identified.

I'm stressing this not because it's so difficult to do but because failing to do so is a major cause of pain and problems. In fact, not having the right team in place is a top reason why companies fail with Amazon.

Doing this right up front or before major problems happen is much easier than trying to fix problems later. Without any more convincing, here is what you want to put in place to manage the Amazon account.

The Optimal Organizational Structure

So far in this book, we covered how important Amazon could be to your business and strategies and tactics that will set you up to win in the short and long term. Now it makes sense to go into the resources you need to execute a plan.

Depending on your organization's size, you probably already have most, if not all, of these resources within your current organization. But before we start executing, it's necessary to identify the key roles and any gaps and to assign responsibilities.

Three distinct groups are needed to make up the Amazon team.

1. Account Management

Account management resources do the day-to-day work with Amazon and execute everything outlined in this book. These would become your organization's Amazon experts, and the needs here are unique to Amazon. Ideal candidates for this group are tech savvy and good at sales or marketing. Some companies have e-commerce roles or salespeople who can do this work.

2. Sales Functions

The second category is more of a traditional sales function that you would need for any large customer. Orders must be processed and filled. Decisions must be made regarding pricing, investment, and profitability. Product content must be created.

3. Cross-Functional Support

The final category is supporting existing resources within your company. Key areas include marketing, product development, finance, and operations.

We highlight these three different roles to really stress that there is more work than just a traditional sales role with a typical customer.

Here are the major responsibilities for each role:

Account Management	Sales Related	Cross Functional Support
• Product setup and maintenance	• Sales Operations	• Product
• Optimization / improvements	• Customer Service	• Marketing
• Lead initiatives within company to improve performance	• Account P&L	• Sales Operations
	• Content Development	• eCommerce
		• Operations
		• Finance

The account management responsibilities are the most specific to Amazon. Account managers will handle the work that will make the account successful by implementing the strategies and tactics presented in this book.

That said, the other two roles also have Amazon-specific knowledge and requirements due to Amazon's demanding operational requirements and the scale at which they execute.

It can be a challenge for these functions to develop the Amazon knowledge they need.

Especially when starting out, another challenge is that there is a disproportionate amount of up-front work. It can be difficult for a resource with other responsibilities to execute the volume of work.

There are high-level strategic elements as well as many more tactical tasks to complete. Business decisions must be made regarding product pricing and launch strategy. Then there is the tactical effort of loading all your products. Each of these is a significant amount of work.

And then there is training—your order management team needs to be trained on how to process Amazon orders, and there are special fulfillment requirements for your operations team.

All of that must be done before selling your first item.

This is true when implementing tactics for high growth. Amazon accounts require active management, and growth requires developing a strategy, identifying and planning tactics, and executing them.

For accounts of any size, this can easily require one or more full-time employees at certain times. And that assumes these employees already have the knowledge they need to execute efficiently. Launching on Amazon is not a learn-on-the-job type of effort if you want to grow.

How to Implement This

Although we have seen companies launch and grow Amazon successfully using in-house resources, many of our clients come to us after attempting to do this on their own and failing. The number one mistake that we see is companies underestimating the amount of work and technical knowledge needed to be successful.

Here is what we would recommend to avoid their mistakes. It's an organizational structure that works well when you want to invest and get results on Amazon. This works for companies just getting started and companies looking to take their performance to the next level.

The key is assigning one person to lead the effort who has the right business authority and capabilities and then providing them with enough resources to execute.

The Amazon leader should have overall ownership of the Amazon account. This means that they own the profit and loss and can make pricing and budget decisions. They would be accountable for delivering the top-line sales and profitability targets.

The amount of time the Amazon leader would need to devote to the work depends on the amount of support they have. It could be as small as 10 percent of their time if they work with a high-quality, full-service/marketing rep agency.

If your company does not want to partner with an outside firm, you can still be successful. The Amazon leader would need to be more familiar with the Amazon platform and know how to implement the business strategies. Realistically, it would be a 25 percent or more commitment on their part. They would also need internal support to execute when there is work that must be implemented. Requirements will vary, but it could easily be at least one full-time employee with an e-commerce background (more technical and marketing focused) at times.

If the Amazon leader does not have some type of support, they will likely fail. In the best case, the sales and growth would be a fraction of what it could be with the support the account needs. More likely, they'll become extremely frustrated as they recognize that they cannot do everything they need to on their own. Additionally, small issues will fester into larger ones that compound. This is when companies usually call us.

Companies like ours, Mantaro Partners, can help with both the management and the execution portions of the work. We can assist the Amazon leader by providing them with high-level strategic guidance on how to best grow their Amazon account. And we can provide the experienced resources necessary to execute.

The needs of the account will change over time.

Once an account is up and running, the needs shift from onboarding to growth and optimizing. This stage is where cross-functional support is critically important, as all the simple problems are fixed and larger opportunities will be pursued that typically cross functional implications.

It's still important to have a single leader in charge of the account, but there is also typically a need for light project management to coordinate the efforts. If done internally, the Amazon leader can often perform both functions.

It's worth mentioning that even companies that partner with outside experts (like us) for this work often eventually bring it in-house by building up an internal team to take over this work. Over time, internal knowledge increases, and at a certain point, the size of the account justifies internally resourcing the work needed to grow and maintain it.

We've worked with manufacturers through this entire process, from launching companies on Amazon, through their growth phases, and then as they transition to bring the management capabilities in-house. We have successfully transitioned the Amazon work to an internal team. Our philosophy here is to support your business in the way that makes the most sense for you, and companies go through an evolution with respect to the needs they have when working with Amazon.

At all phases, top organizations focus on clear definitions of success. The next section outlines the key metrics we use to ensure that the management of Amazon is on track. These metrics are important whether you manage Amazon in-house or work with a company like us.

Measuring Success as a Business Owner

Online channels and Amazon in particular give you near real-time data on your product performance. Here is what we recommend that you monitor on a regular basis to track your performance.

All these metrics should be tracked in aggregate, at minimum. It also makes sense to track metrics at product categories and even individual products for bestsellers and strategic products.

Sales Growth

This may seem obvious, but some Amazon specifics are worth mentioning. First, you want to measure the growth at the point of sale—from Amazon's perspective. For vendors, this comes directly from their reporting of shipped cost of goods sold (COGS). For sellers, this comes from the business reports.

You should track this on a monthly basis. Although there will be some variability month to month, you should expect, in general, for sales to increase month over month. If your sales trend is flat or decreasing, it's a sign that there could be an issue.

Given that Amazon is growing, your sales should grow year over year.

I would recommend getting a sense of how your sales growth is performing against your category or key competitors as well as against Amazon overall. A 5 percent year-over-year growth may be good for a brick-and-mortar customer, but it likely means you're losing share on Amazon.

If you're actively managing your Amazon channel, your sales should be growing at least as fast as Amazon.

Profitability

Understanding account- and product-level profitability is critically important. What you sell your products for on Amazon is not what you get paid. Amazon has various deductions that they take from each sale. Additionally, promotional programs like advertising are a real cost that must be factored into your profit and loss.

It's an easy mistake to make assumptions about these costs and to focus just on sales revenue and growth. Amazon is more than happy to have you concentrate on sales growth rather than on your profitability. Some believe their reports and dashboards are purposely designed to keep you fixated on top-line growth rather than on factors that could impact your profitability.

It's important to calculate and monitor actual profitability for two reasons:

- Because it's easy to buy growth with advertising and other promotional services, you want to make sure that you're buying profitable growth. Every product should have its own profit and loss to ensure that it's net profitable.
- Amazon payments and transaction details are extremely complex. It's not uncommon for Amazon to make mistakes in their billing of fees or for your account to accrue unexpected fees. These fees can erode profitability, and the only way to be aware of this is to actively monitor and track account profit and loss as well.

This is such a big issue that there is an entire industry of companies that audit Amazon receipts and work with Amazon on an ongoing basis to dispute fees and shortages.

We routinely find five-, six-, and even seven-figure charges on accounts that are surprises to manufacturers. Some of these are refundable, others have strategies to mitigate, and some are required costs of business that were just not anticipated. In all cases, these fees impact profitability, so it's critical to be aware of them so that you can make the best business decisions.

Inventory Levels

The third key metric to track is inventory levels. There are two inventories you must monitor—inventory at your warehouse and inventory at Amazon.

Inventory at your warehouse is simpler to address. You probably already have more than enough to service the Amazon business today. But because Amazon can grow much faster than traditional customers, you must ensure that you maintain sufficient levels in the future as Amazon becomes a more significant business.

This is particularly challenging due to how Amazon orders from vendors. Amazon orders can vary considerably week to week. It's not uncommon for Amazon orders to double (or half) one week to the next, so just tracking historical purchases to predict future purchases is not enough. You need to account for Amazon's inventory changes and expected demand shifts and potentially increase your safety stock to handle the variability.

Managing your warehouse inventory can also become complex for sellers. To be successful, you need to keep a constant stream of products going to Amazon fulfillment centers. The amount of inventory that you must keep at Amazon and the lead time it requires will probably put demands on your inventory management that your other channels do not.

The second aspect is inventory at Amazon. This cannot be ignored, even if it's technically not your responsibility as a vendor, because you lose if Amazon stocks out. Amazon stockouts cause lost sales and lost sales momentum—making the virtuous cycle work against you. You need to keep an eye on how much inventory is at Amazon and available for sale.

The goal is for there to always be products listed on Amazon and available for sale.

Sellers are directly responsible for forecasting and maintaining the inventory at Amazon. This becomes a critical activity to keep products in stock and selling. If you do it wrong, you lose out on the sale and momentum drops. We recommend ensuring regular shipments into Amazon so that there is more than enough inventory at Amazon and in transit.

A challenge for sellers is that Amazon receiving is highly variable, and you never want to stockout. The trick is to maintain sufficient safety stock while not paying too much in inbound shipping and inventory storage fees.

Vendors have an advantage here, as Amazon manages inventory levels for inventory that they buy. If Amazon stocks out of a product today, they will likely place a reorder in a few days (if they don't already have the product in transit). That said, Amazon's forecasting is not perfect, and glitches happen that could result in significant stockouts if you don't take action.

Amazon's attitude with regard to inventory is to make a good effort. If they stockout of your products, the Amazon customers will be forced to buy your competitor's product. This situation harms you much more than Amazon, so it's critical to monitor their inventory and to take action if their stock levels get too low.

Vendors have tools like the Born to Run program that allows them to give Amazon additional guidance on what product (and how much) to buy.

More Advanced Metrics

If all you do is track sales, profits, and inventory levels in aggregate and at the product level, you will have all the metrics you need to manage and grow your business. Knowing these metrics at the product level puts you ahead of 95 percent of manufacturers out there.

There are other metrics that are useful for more advanced insights. They include the following:

- Traffic reports ensure that the traffic you're getting converts appropriately and identifies under converting pages.
- The conversion rate is either provided or can be computed and identifies changes in customer purchasing behavior and products with issues.
- Amazon's net pure profit margin can help vendors identify product profitability issues.
- Market share is calculated by combining your sales with a market analysis to determine how much of the addressable market you're capturing.

Know your numbers and you can control your destiny.

Monitoring Is a Key Component

The metrics mentioned from the previous section let you know how your business is performing. Tracking them over time (and watching the numbers go up) gives you insight into what is working on Amazon and that you are winning against your competition. These metrics will also let you plan for the future as you get a better sense of what is possible.

Amazon's metrics can be tracked at the account and product levels, giving you a very granular view of your business. Any large Amazon account is actually a combination of several distinct businesses—groups of products that are winning and groups of products that are losing. Product-level metrics let you identify and hopefully fix losers.

But there is a way to identify potential losers before they start impacting your top or bottom line. This early-warning signal is a critical but often overlooked aspect of managing your Amazon business.

The early-warning signal comes from regularly monitoring your key listing pages. You should check your bestsellers daily to make sure that the page exists, that there is a buy box, and that the product is being sold by the seller(s) you expect.

This sounds simple, even trivial. But you'd be surprised by the number of times we've audited accounts and found major bestsellers that have just stopped selling . . . and no one knew about it.

The dirty little secret is that Amazon doesn't really care. Sometimes they'll email a manufacturer about an issue, but in many cases the product just becomes unsellable. After all, they have the traffic, and at the end of the day, Amazon wins regardless of whether the shopper buys your product or your competitor's.

But you obviously do care. And you want all your products available with active product pages. That is why monitoring your listings is critical.

This can be done manually, where someone on your team visits bestselling pages daily or weekly looking for issues. Or it can be done automatically with a service.

Basic monitoring typically ensures that the product is buyable only from specific sellers. More advanced monitoring can ensure that the hard work you put into marketing and listing optimization remains alive and doesn't get overwritten via an unauthorized page change.

As your business with Amazon grows, monitoring is a cheap insurance policy that helps protect your investment.

* * * *

Whew! We've covered a lot of ground in the book so far—everything from Amazon myths, benefits, and market size to optimizing listing pages and generating traffic to grow your business.

And this chapter discussed how to manage that business—from the organizational structure to measuring success and monitoring.

Altogether, this comprises all the basics you need to start winning on Amazon. This is the exact playbook we use to build our clients' businesses. If you stopped right here and started implementing everything you learned, you could quickly build a seven-figure business from scratch or double an existing Amazon business.

But we're not stopping here—there's more! I really want you to be successful. In the next chapter, I'll cover some common challenges that you're likely to encounter as you execute this plan . . . and how to overcome them.

CHAPTER 11

TRAPS YOU'LL FACE ONCE YOU'RE SELLING ON AMAZON (AND HOW TO AVOID THEM)

The road to Amazon success is paved in gold, but even the best products executed by the best team will encounter some challenges. Whether they're just bumps in the road or deadly pitfalls depends on how well you anticipate the traps and mitigate their effects.

Amazon is very much a learn-as-you-go process. As such, it's often hard to anticipate the challenges that you may encounter, and this is especially true as you grow. The issues you solve as a $1 million brand don't necessarily prepare you for the issues you'll encounter as a $5 million or a $10 million brand.

As Donald Rumsfeld likes to say, "You don't know what you don't know." And this is especially true with Amazon, where there can always be a new and interesting trap right around the corner.

In this chapter, I'll outline some of the more common challenges you may encounter. The goal is to give you some insights into how to recognize some common issues that trip up companies and how to solve them and continue your success.

Why Amazon Sells Your Products for a Loss

Believe it or not, Amazon will sometimes sell products for a loss. They will do this if your list price is too low or if they notice other retailers selling the same product for less. Amazon will scrape other online retailers and even have live shoppers who go into large brick-and-mortar stores to check pricing.

If they see your products sold on a large retailer for a lower price, Amazon will match it. And if you're a seller and Amazon can't do that because you control the retail price, Amazon will instead suppress your pages until you "voluntarily" lower the price. They do this regardless of profitability.

They may also sell your product for a loss if they're overstocked. A below-market price is the best way to move their excess inventory.

Why would you care if Amazon wants to sell for a loss? The problem with Amazon losing money is that they won't allow it to go on forever. Eventually, Amazon will stop selling money-losing products.

Amazon has an acronym for it—CRAP (can't realize a profit). And if your product CRAPs out, Amazon will stop selling it—forever. It's virtually impossible to get them to sell it again.

We've worked with a well-known household brand whose leading SKU sells for $2.99 in Walmart. Amazon sold the exact same product and matched the in-store Walmart pricing. This went on for months, and during that time Amazon lost millions of dollars on that SKU. And then one day the orders stopped. Amazon crapped it out and never bought it again.

This only affects vendors, and you want to avoid this as much as possible because it's basically irreversible. It's not always avoidable, but you can usually anticipate which products are at risk to CRAP out. Products with low Amazon margin (retail—cost) and low retail price (generally less than $10) are at highest risk.

We recommend first identifying at-risk products and then determining whether there is a path to improve Amazon's profitability. The two "easiest" ways are to break the price match by no longer selling to the Amazon competitor or lowering your costs. (We put "easiest" in quotes because these are easy solutions to outline but hard to actually implement.)

If you cannot improve Amazon's profitability, you want to identify a way to protect the revenue once the product CRAPs out. This can be done by identifying (or creating) a replacement product that has better economics for Amazon than the existing one. You would then want to transfer as much of the market share to the new product once the CRAP out happens.

External ID and Product Barcoding Issues

This is the second potentially irreversible pitfall. Amazon uses UPCs, EANs, and GTINs to identify most products. The UPC/EAN/GTIN is the product's external ID from Amazon's perspective, and it must be on the product as a barcode. The reason for this is that Amazon's entire warehouse system operates exclusively on product barcodes, and the barcode is the map that connects a physical product to a specific listing page. The association between the barcode and the listing page is created when the product is first added to Amazon.

The problem occurs if the association turns out to be wrong. Let's say that you make a mistake when creating a new listing and provide Amazon with the wrong barcode information. Or the wrong barcode was printed on the product label. Or the barcode changes due to production reasons.

Or one of your customers decided to list one of your products and used the wrong UPC. Or used your UPC for the wrong product.

You get it—there are a lot of different ways that the wrong barcode could be assigned to a product.

Regardless of the scenario, incorrect barcoding can cause huge issues. Some of these issues could make your product unsellable, especially if you are a vendor. Another possible impact of incorrect barcoding is that your warehouse team would have to manually sticker each item with a replacement barcode. This is often cost prohibitive.

This happens because Amazon receives products automatically with no human intervention. They process items according to their understanding of the barcode, regardless of what is actually there. So wrong barcodes can lead to products not being received or Amazon thinking something else was received. And if products are not received properly, you are not going to get paid properly.

Depending on the exact scenario, it can be virtually impossible to get Amazon to fix the situation. Amazon views external ID barcoding as etched in stone.

The best solution when it comes to barcoding is to get it right the first time. Double-check UPCs and external IDs prior to loading the product. Make sure your cases do not have the same barcoding as the individual units. Physically inspect the product if there is any doubt and double-check any submission that includes external IDs.

And if you find yourself in a situation where you have corrupted external IDs or products, either change your products' barcodes or get professional help. The exact solution, if there is one, will depend on the specifics of your situation.

A Product with No Sales

You have a product with an established market. You list it on Amazon and get . . . no sales.

There are two major causes for this, and they go back to the principles of growing Amazon sales—traffic and conversion. Most likely either the page is not getting traffic or the page does not convert.

First, traffic. Is your page getting traffic? Are you advertising it? You should be able to see traffic reports and advertising metrics. If traffic is going to your page, you should expect sales.

Also make sure that you can find your product when you search for it using your brand and title. It's possible that a perfectly good product is searched incorrectly by Amazon.

Once you have confirmed that your product page is getting traffic, it's time to look at the actual page.

Second, conversion. Check whether you have a compelling product page and offer. Do your product page and main image do the product justice? What about the product's price? Ensure that the product is offered for sale with immediate Prime shipping at a good retail price.

High pricing is a top reason for no sales. If the price is high relative to comparable products on Amazon, then do not expect it to sell. If you feel that your product is premium relative to other products on Amazon, make sure that the page feels premium compared to the Amazon competition. You want your product's pricing to fit within the Amazon market made up of your competition both on and off Amazon. Some products have economics that just are not competitive on Amazon. (Pro tip: Don't sell fifty-pound bags of cement on Amazon.)

You should also ensure that the page has the information needed to convert shoppers. Does it have the necessary information to motivate shoppers to buy? How does it compare against your competition (on and off Amazon)? Your product page should be comparable in content and quality to other similar products on Amazon. Have a fresh set of eyes review your product page and get their feedback.

Build It and They Will Come

This trap is a variation of the one discussed in the previous section.

It's worth mentioning because it's very common. A manufacturer launches a new product, adds it to Amazon, and gets no sales. It's very demoralizing but entirely predictable.

Adding a product to Amazon doesn't automatically get you sales. Just because you built it doesn't mean anyone will come to the page and buy. In many cases, a new product page will get zero organic visitors.

In short, you need a plan to drive traffic. And you should have the plan figured out prior to adding a product to Amazon. That way you can add the product and maximize the sales momentum right out of the gate. See chapter 10 for a summary of the steps you should take.

Bad Product Feedback

You want to maintain above-average feedback on your products. Feedback will vary a bit by market, but in general most of your products should have at least three and a half stars.

You should monitor your product's feedback. It will give you a heads-up on potential quality issues and could provide you with insights into how to market your products better.

If you consistently get bad feedback, you have a missed expectation. Either there is wrong or missing information on your listing page or your product is just too expensive. Check your product page to make sure that the feedback is properly addressed.

The missed expectation can also be about the value for the price. There are no such things as bad products, only products that are priced too high. A $100 product that gets two stars can be a four-star $70 product. Or a five-star $50 product.

And don't worry about every piece of bad feedback. The best product will occasionally get negative feedback from angry users. Or from good faith users who had an honest bad experience. This last type of feedback can actually help sell your product, as it gives buyers a balanced perspective on your item, which may make it seem more trustworthy.

You can sometimes remove reviews that are against terms of service (such as shipping issues) by emailing community-help@amazon.com with the details.

Selling Your Products for a Loss

We covered when Amazon sells your product for a loss. Even worse is when you sell your products to Amazon for a loss.

It sounds crazy, but trust me—it happens. If you aren't calculating your profitability at the product level, there's a chance you may have products that are losing money.

It's easy to focus on sales growth and product growth and not calculate your fully loaded margin at the product level.

We've seen scenarios where the manufacturer would be better throwing the product away than selling it. Here are some actual examples:

- The manufacturer calculated profitability based on what they quoted Amazon—not on what Amazon paid them after contractual discounts.
- The product was packaged incorrectly and was manually labeled by Amazon. Amazon charges for this, and it causes receiving issues in which Amazon would receive less than what was shipped. After the shortages and label charges, the product lost money.
- The manufacturer ran their own advertising and focused only on sales and on the account-level advertising metrics. This hid the fact that they were significantly overadvertising on certain products to drive revenue at the expense of profit. They had a negative net margin on key products.

I could easily give another dozen examples. Tracking sales is easy, but understanding your profitability at the product level can be hard.

The only solution is to calculate profitability at the product level and to allocate all direct costs to the product—discounts, accruals, inbound shipping, allowances, promotions, advertising, shortages, fines, chargebacks, returns, and so on.

An added benefit is that once you do this, you also know the products that contribute the most to your profitability and can adjust your marketing to maximize what really matters—profit and dollars in the bank.

Amazon Is Violating My MAP Policy or Undercutting My Other Retailers

If you are a vendor, Amazon gets to set the retail price. Some manufacturers worry that Amazon will set the pricing so low that their other retail customers will not be able to compete.

Usually these concerns are unfounded. And if you implement the advice in the chapter on pricing, you can "encourage" Amazon to price properly. However, in some cases, Amazon may price too low from the manufacturer's perspective.

When this happens, it is worth figuring out why Amazon is pricing as they are. The most common reason that Amazon sees another one of your retailers also selling for a low price.

It's rare for Amazon to be the root cause of a pricing issue. More typically, another retailer is causing it and Amazon just brings visibility to it. Amazon will price match any other online retailer it sees or even another seller on the Amazon site.

As we mentioned elsewhere, Amazon may initiate price cuts and be the source of the low price if they are overstocked. Ensuring that you have a high converting page and bringing more traffic to the page can help to fix that situation.

We have a client that does 90 percent of their online business through Amazon. (This is true for many of our clients.) They have a MAP policy, but one of their most popular SKUs was being priced well below MAP on Amazon. They found out about it when other customers complained to them. It was an embarrassing situation for them because they were known for aggressively policing their MAP policy.

Thankfully, they understood how Amazon prices and didn't turn off one of their most profitable accounts. They had us investigate the pricing issue, and we discovered that Amazon was price matching one of their other very small e-retailer customers. That e-retailer sold an inconsequential amount of their product but did so at heavily discounted pricing.

Because the smaller e-retailer was corrupting their biggest e-commerce channel, the manufacturer closed the e-retailer's account. The pricing on Amazon returned back to normal within a couple of days.

In rare cases, Amazon does incorrectly price products on its own, but I would always recommend looking at market and competitive pricing first. In almost all cases, Amazon retail pricing can be fixed.

If all else fails, you can always stop selling a SKU until the issue is resolved.

Spending Too Little on Advertising

There are two potential pitfalls with advertising. Spending too little or spending too much. Well-run accounts rarely spend too much (and since you have this book, you are likely a well-run account). So we'll focus on how to know if you are spending too little on advertising.

Let's first handle the easy case. If you're spending zero dollars on advertising, you're spending too little. You need to spend more because you're not maximizing your traffic or your sales or your profits. We've never seen an account that would be worse off top line and bottom line from advertising.

But let's assume that you are spending some advertising on your products. First, you should have a good handle on your key metrics—ACoS/ROAS and TACoS. Second, you should know your profit margin.

You then need to make a decision on how aggressive you want to be. We have aggressive clients who will let their ACoS = net profit margin. In this situation, when you sell a product from advertising, 100 percent of the net profit on that sale paid for advertising.

Although you don't make money on that particular sale, you're maximizing the ranking benefits you get from advertising. This should increase the number of organic sales you get. As long as your TACoS is reasonable, you are aggressively maximizing your reach on Amazon. This can be an extremely profitable strategy for bold competitors.

Other clients insist on having every sale be profitable. In this case, ACoS is < net profit. This is a less aggressive but perfectly acceptable approach. The key is to have an idea of what is an acceptable amount to pay for advertised sales (ACoS) and overall (TACoS).

Once you've set an upper threshold for ACoS, you then want to make sure you're maximizing your opportunities within that boundary. There is no right or wrong answer—like we said, it really depends on your product economics and business environment.

But once you have those guidelines, it's easy to diagnose if you're spending too little on advertising. Here are some questions to ask yourself:

- Do you have sponsored product campaigns running on all products? If not, then you're leaving sales on the table.
- Are you hitting daily budgets? If yes, then your budgets are too low and you're leaving sales on the table.
- Do you tune them regularly? If not, then you're not optimizing your ads and are leaving sales on the table.
- Are you under your ACoS goal? Then you can spend more on individual products.
- Are you under your TACoS goal? Then you should expand the ad types used and lean into the ones that work particularly well.

Once you get above a few thousand dollars a month, advertising usually requires some specialized knowledge. We recommend using software or an agency to ensure the most effective use of your budget. There are many decent advertising agencies out there that can help put together a comprehensive advertising strategy for you. (And we even do it as part of the overall service we provide our clients.)

Don't Set and Forget—You Need to Actively Manage Amazon

Some manufacturers believe that once Amazon is set up, they're done. Although some customers and channels may be like that, Amazon certainly is not.

Amazon requires active management and ongoing maintenance. There are two primary reasons for this:

1. *The environment is constantly changing.* Your business is growing and with it there are new challenges and opportunities. Additionally, the market is always changing with new competitors and new pricing.

2. *Amazon changes (and breaks occasionally).* Amazon grows fast. They add new features, tweak their algorithms, and even break things fairly regularly. They do their best to inform their

suppliers, but someone needs to keep an eye on things to make sure everything continues to work.

We recently were asked to audit a large manufacturer's account. They started selling on Amazon about six years ago. Here is how their sales looked:

Year over Year Growth

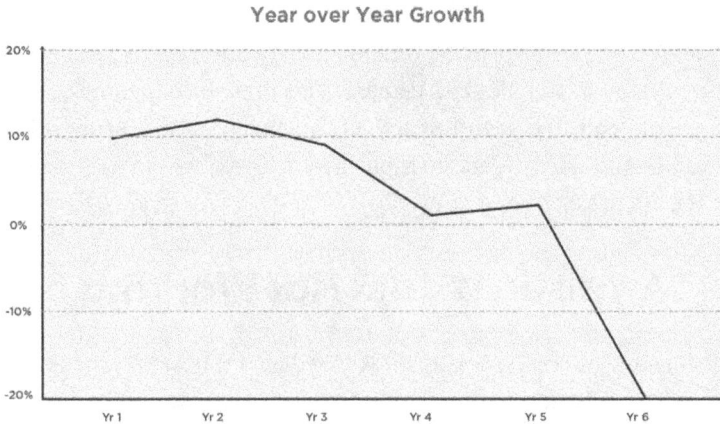

In their opinion, everything was great in the first five years. They only called us because they didn't understand why sales were suddenly dropping.

The sales were dropping because their listing pages were no longer competitive. There were dozens of minor issues that all negatively impacted sales.

In reality, they had been losing market share for years, but the market was growing quickly enough that it basically had a neutral impact. But in the last year, the competitive environment shifted enough that virtually all the sales transitioned away from their pages and they finally saw a sales drop.

They thought their problem was just a 20 percent drop in sales. But their real problem was several years of lost sales due to neglect—their sales would have been at least two times their current rate if they had actively managed their account.

Active management means implementing the tactics in this book. And then monitoring everything to make sure the tactics worked. And then repeating the process again as things change.

This doesn't necessarily take a lot of time (especially if you outsource much of the work), but it does mean that your marketing evolves over time and that sales should keep up or exceed the Amazon market as a whole.

Active management is the difference between 5 to 10 percent year-over-year growth and 20 to 50 percent. This growth compounds, so over a couple of years, the payoff of actively managing your account is huge. You can realistically expect your business to grow two to five times the size. It's dramatic.

"Amazon Is Just Not Working."

Some manufacturers, especially those that do not follow the advice in this book, run into issues working with Amazon. They get exasperated and want to quit or make a drastic change. "Amazon is too difficult," "We're not getting any sales," or "The juice is just not worth the squeeze" are common ways they express it.

Although I think that almost any manufacturer can be successful on Amazon, ultimately that is your choice. What I always ask companies that are ready to quit is whether they have the information they need to make an informed choice.

Knowing that Amazon is not working or is too difficult is not enough. That is just the symptom of a problem. It takes some digging to understand the root cause and then some Amazon expertise to develop a solution.

I worked with a large publicly traded company a few years back that was ready to quit Amazon. Their complaint was that Amazon wasn't paying them consistently. And Amazon suffered because they weren't receiving all the products the company shipped. The company didn't know why this was happening but was smart enough to reach out to have me investigate before they decided what to do.

It turned out there was a technical incompatibility between Amazon's ordering system and the company's ordering system. Fixing it would require implementing a formal IT project. They couldn't justify the investment that year, so they decided to pause Amazon until IT budgets freed up.

Last year they had us do an updated market assessment. Based on that, they were able to fund the project and relaunched on Amazon. With the root issue fixed, Amazon is receiving properly and paying on time. The company is very happy with the growth and has started to dominate their market on Amazon.

This story had a happy ending, but the point is that if things aren't working, you first need to figure out why and then decide what you want to do about it. Focusing on the surface level is not enough.

This book (or our firm) can help you diagnose what is going on and provide recommendations to fix it. But that doesn't guarantee that you will be able to or want to fix it. In the publicly traded company example, it took more than two years before they were able to prioritize the needed changes. Most companies have significantly fewer resources than them. But when things are not working, you must understand the true root cause. Once you know that, you can then make an informed decision on how to proceed.

Wanting to Switch to Seller Central

A variation of the previous pitfall is wanting to switch to Amazon Seller Central.

If things are going badly, a manufacturer may consider quitting Amazon. But if you are a vendor, they will typically first consider switching to Seller Central.

As a quick refresher, vendors sell products directly to Amazon through a web app called Vendor Central. Sellers make products available for sale through Seller Central.

Seller Central typically comes up when a manufacturer is having problems with profitability, pricing, or fines (charge-backs). Exasperated, they start searching the internet for solutions and hear about how much better Seller Central is. It's not a coincidence that the source of how great Seller Central is comes from a consultant who sells services to move vendors to Seller Central.

Several semitrue claims will be made—you can set your own prices on Seller Central, it is much easier and flexible, there are no fines! They make it sound wonderful. Why would anyone want to stay on Vendor Central?

It's all a sales pitch, and there are no magic bullets.

We've been brought into these conversations more than once. In almost every case, two things are true:

1. The root problems are not being addressed.
2. The recommendation is self-serving—the consultant advising them to switch really only works in and understands Seller Central. They do not understand Vendor Central and how to solve problems there.

Although there are specific situations where being a seller is better than being a vendor (or vice versa), in many cases, switching only temporarily solves the symptoms of larger root problems. If the root problems are not addressed, at best the switch only postpones failure. As we mentioned in the last section, it's critical to identify and solve the root issues. Doing this makes your business strong and profitable in both the short term and the long term.

Almost every strong Amazon business can thrive on either Seller Central or Vendor Central. Our firm helps manufacturers succeed on both platforms. Each has their trade-offs, and one may be a better fit for you than the other. But if there are fundamental issues with your Amazon business, switching will not solve them.

Can't Raise Prices as a Vendor

"But, Nate, we can't get a price increase through. We can't keep selling to Amazon for a loss, and Seller Central will let us set our own pricing."

Technically this is true. If you must raise your prices and can't get a cost increase through on Vendor Central, then your only option to keep access to the Amazon market is Seller Central.

But this situation illustrates the concept from the previous sections that a root issue is likely not being addressed.

If you can't raise prices, your account is either too small to get Amazon's attention or not profitable enough (for Amazon). If you are too small, your cost increase requests will be ignored, and if you are not profitable, they will be denied (to prevent Amazon from losing more margin).

These are root issues that must be solved before you need a cost increase. The previous chapters outline how to address both.

But even in this situation, Seller Central is not a miracle cure. If Amazon has profitability issues, they could be driven by competitive market pricing problems. The Amazon marketplace fair pricing policy may force the same profitability issues that Amazon deals with directly onto you, if you want to maintain sales.

That is because Amazon forces competitive pricing even in Seller Central. If you want to sell your widget for $39.99 but Walmart is selling it for $30, Amazon will suppress your listing if you do not price match Walmart. This is why it is critical to understand Amazon's profitability and identify issues like this before Amazon's profitability issues start impacting you directly.

More importantly, you want to think about raising prices before you have to raise prices. You want to ensure that Amazon has enough margin so that when you go to negotiate a price increase six months from now, you don't get major pushback. If you wait until the day of the negotiation to worry about Amazon's profitability, it's too late to do anything about it.

Ultimately, cost increases are part of the ongoing management of your account. Ensuring that they happen regularly and that Amazon has sufficient profitability to be willing to raise your costs is something that should be implemented as part of your ongoing work.

Expecting Amazon to Grow Your Business for You

Some manufacturers assume that there is an Amazon buyer or merchandiser that makes product decisions, promotes products, and manages the product pages.

This is not really the case. You may have a human contact you can talk to, but usually their scope is very limited, such as managing a product category or selling services rather than merchandising or promoting your products. Amazon is a self-serve platform and expects you to be the primary advocate for your products.

For example, vendor managers care about the number of products offered, the sales growth, and the margin contribution—at the category level. They don't really care about your products and will spend very little time, if any, looking at your account.

And when they do, it's more focused on the overall account than on the merchandising of any given product. Vendor managers' ability to impact products, brands, and accounts is extremely limited because most internal functions at Amazon are automated.

There are other contacts at Amazon, but their involvement is usually extremely limited in scope. Here are some that you may encounter and where they can be helpful:

- *Advertising account managers:* They are useful in helping you set up advertising campaigns. But you are responsible for ongoing optimization and monitoring.
- *White glove onboarding:* This is helpful in setting you up with minimally viable pages. Once they're gone, you'll need to manage and grow the business on your own.
- *Premium support services:* You can pay for Amazon's premium support services. They can be very helpful in resolving problems and can provide some proactive monitoring. If you have a strong strategy to grow your Amazon business, they can be useful to help make it happen.

At the end of the day, Amazon provides the tools and leaves it up to you to decide how to use them. Your success (or failure) is completely up to you and the team you assemble.

Focusing on the Pretty Rather Than on the Important

"I am convinced that about one-half the money I spend on advertising is wasted, but I have never been able to decide which half."

This famous quote is attributed to John Wannamaker, a pioneer in marketing who died in 1922.

Of course, the modern-day follow-up is that with e-commerce, you can know which half is wasted since you measure everything. And we covered key metrics in chapter 9.

But I think the quote still applies today even in e-commerce. Although we can measure a lot, there are still many important things in marketing that you cannot easily measure. One is the aesthetics of your marketing materials.

You want your product pages to look good. But more important than that is for your product pages to be effective. From an aesthetic perspective, effective means pages that match your branding and pages that do not look bad.

Meeting these criteria can result in high converting pages. It may not be pretty or fancy, but in many cases it doesn't need to be to drive sales.

What I'm trying to communicate is that you want to focus your time with Amazon on tactics that matter and that drive conversion. Most are outlined in this book.

The pretty aspects of marketing are often more fun and certainly more visible. Sexy images. Great graphic design. Custom fonts. Highly stylized content. Social media marketing.

Don't get me wrong—pretty is great. But pretty doesn't always drive sales. Unsexy steps do: having your product be sellable, at a good price, with good content to accurately and compellingly sell it.

As I said before, if you do that, you'll easily be in the top 10 percent of products on Amazon.

Taking It Personally

I've alluded to this before, but virtually every product-level decision that Amazon makes is done by a computer algorithm. There are no shoppers who decide what products to buy or merchandisers that pick which products to feature in a category. It's all done by machine, automatically.

The people you will talk to at Amazon, if you do talk to anyone, primarily are there to help you better interface with how the machine works and to help you (and Amazon) when things with the machine algorithm go wrong.

This is very different from what many manufacturers are used to. You potentially have relationships with many of your customers where you have built up goodwill over the years. Many of my clients travel to visit their customers and have become friends with them over the years. Even if your business is not like that, most likely you can pick up the phone and talk to someone who can make decisions if there are issues.

These concepts do not exist in the same sense at Amazon. There is no relationship with the algorithm. You can be a profitable account for ten years, but that history doesn't matter if you are not profitable today. And there is often no one you can call on at Amazon if there is an issue. You submit a written ticket, and the problem is dealt with by a one-size-fits-all procedure.

Amazon operates in an extremely transactional way. People who are used to relationships with more human-based interactions can find this to be a hard adjustment. Amazon makes decisions based on whether it furthers Amazon's goals, and that's it.

From time to time, Amazon's decisions would not make sense if looked at from a partnership perspective with a normal human. If a human was involved in the decision, that human probably doesn't really understand your products and was just following a documented standard operating procedure. It's really frustrating when a human acts like a mindless computer.

You must remember that Amazon is an algorithm (made up of computers and humans) and that algorithms do not have feelings or maintain relationships. So don't take it personally.

The good news is that algorithms can be understood. Once you know how an algorithm works, you know what you need to do to get the outputs you want. And that is exactly what this book is—a manual that outlines what levers to pull on the Amazon machine to get the outputs you want to succeed in your business!

CHAPTER 12

REVIEWING THE AMAZON PLAYBOOK: HOW TO WIN ON AMAZON STEP-BY-STEP

We've covered a tremendous amount of information in this book. I shared all the basics you need to know to achieve massive sustainable growth on Amazon. It might seem overwhelming, so the goal of this chapter is to bring it all together in a concise action plan that you can implement within your organization.

Think of this chapter as your Amazon project plan that kicks off today. We'll outline exactly what you need to do to start a successful Amazon project in your organization. In fact, much of this is taken directly from the internal implementation plans that we use when working with new clients.

You may be new to Amazon, and if so, we have outlined all the steps for you. Or your products may have been on Amazon for years and you want to supercharge your sales growth. In that case, just skip the steps you've already mastered to have a plan suited just for you.

Either way, this is the process that we apply to our clients to achieve above double-digit, above-average growth that lasts for years.

The Ten Steps to Win on Amazon and Create Perennial Bestsellers

I. Identify and task leadership.

1. Identify the day-to-day owner of Amazon.
2. Identify key organizational stakeholders.
3. Appoint an executive sponsor to keep the organization accountable and to cut through the red tape.

II. Develop goals.

1. Determine an addressable opportunity.
2. Understand the competitive landscape.
3. Set short- and long-term sales and profit goals and incentivize the team to achieve them.

III. Assess the current state.

1. What is the current state of your catalog's sales and marketing materials? How do they compare to the competition?
2. Are your products currently on Amazon? Do the Amazon pages do a good job of representing your products?
3. Do a pricing and profitability analysis to ensure that you have competitive pricing that is profitable.

IV. Implement budgeting and measurement.

1. Determine one-time costs to budget—product launches, content development.
2. Calculate ongoing costs to budget—advertising, promotions. Obtain outside support if needed.
3. Develop your promotional calendar.
4. Set achievable and stretch monthly and yearly growth targets.

V. Set up the account.

1. Select the account type and set it up.
2. Train key team members in order processing and order fulfillment.

VI. Load products.

1. Finalize product pricing.
2. Complete product templates and load products to the account.
3. Load images and merchandise pages as needed.

VII. Launch.

1. Send in initial inventory (Fulfillment by Amazon for sellers, Born to Run for vendors).
2. Turn on backup inventory (Fulfilled by Merchant for sellers, direct fulfillment for vendors).
3. On Amazon: Set up advertising campaigns, kick off promotions, and initiate other launch tactics.
4. Off Amazon: Distribute promotion codes to loyal customers, send email blasts, and create social posts.

VIII. Track performance.

1. Monitor sales, reviews, and search performance.
2. Track account and product profit and loss.
3. Calculate advertising and promotional performance.

IX. Optimization—learn from results and invest in what works.

1. Lean into advertising and promotional tactics that work.
2. Incorporate keywords and feedback into your listing optimization.
3. Improve over time; build on success.
4. Broaden your target markets as you build success.
5. Benchmark against key competitors.

X. Grow.

1. Introduce new products, new niches, and new package quantities and configurations.
2. Identify opportunities to remove costs from the supply chain and provide greater value to end users.
3. Leverage areas of strength such as high traffic products/tactics and bestsellers to grow sales in hidden or emerging opportunities.

Most companies should be able to go from start to launch (step VII) within 90 to 120 days.

The track-optimize-grow phases (steps VIII through X) should go on indefinitely, with typically the strongest results during your first three years of execution.

Amazon Is Predictable: There Is a Recipe for Success

The secret to winning on Amazon is simple. With just three ingredients, you can be guaranteed to have Amazon be one of your best customers.

We sprinkled the recipe throughout the book, but it's worth recapping here:

- *First ingredient:* You need a right to win—good products that people want at good prices.
- *Second ingredient:* You need a plan. That is exactly what this book gives you.
- *Third and last ingredient:* You need a team to implement the plan.

The team is a combination of business-savvy strategic thinkers who can chart a path of success for your business and a scalable team of doers to execute it.

If you have these three ingredients, you have a recipe for success.

Mantaro Partners: We Can Help Your Amazon Business Grow Faster, Easier

I may have mentioned that I run an Amazon consulting and manufacturing rep firm. I might even have mentioned that we have deep experience doing exactly what is described in this book—delivering multiple years of above-average growth for clients at every stage of their Amazon journey.

We've helped manufacturers sell their first product on Amazon. We've launched new product lines.

We've helped established companies double their sales.

We've taken manufacturers ready to quit Amazon and transformed them into happy and successful Amazon suppliers.

We have even helped companies with significant Amazon sales become more self-sufficient by developing their internal capabilities.

We have the resources to grow accounts quickly and the experience to solve problems before they impact the business.

We've put our best advice into this book, with the goal to educate and help as many manufacturers be successful on Amazon as possible. If you have the resources to put what's here into practice, you will be extremely successful on Amazon.

That said, many companies don't have the ability to maximize the Amazon opportunity. Many employees these days are stretched too thin with too many responsibilities. Managing an Amazon business is a time-consuming process.

Additionally, it comes with a learning curve. Not every company has the luxury to invest the time or money to develop in-house Amazon expertise, especially when the account is still relatively small.

Because of this, outsourcing the launch and growth phases can be extremely beneficial. You get the scale and expertise of an organization that sells more than $100 million per year on Amazon on day one for a fraction of the cost. As a result, you grow faster and more profitably, with fewer problems.

This is a blatant commercial for our services, but the fact is that we have significant experience in taking manufacturers from zero to multi-millions in Amazon sales and in taking established manufacturers and unleashing their growth potential.

We have done it in a variety of industries and have delivered success with the same companies over multiple years. We can do the same thing for you—give you more sales and more profit, all the while allowing you to sleep better at night knowing that your Amazon sales are under control.

Our services are not cheap, but our results—in sales and in peace of mind—are impressive and pay for our fees many times over.

If this sounds interesting and if you are a manufacturer with an established history of brick-and-mortar sales, we'd love to chat with you about how we can help.

And if you have the resources to succeed, we are still at your disposal. I really want you to win.

If you have questions about anything in this book, feel free to reach out.

We can discuss your business, your experience with Amazon, and any issues or concerns you have.

As a reader of this book, the goal of the call would be to provide you with actionable next steps—regardless of whether you want to work with us or on your own. We want you to be successful and to have Amazon be one of your biggest and most profitable channels.

Schedule your free, no-obligation consultation at www.mantaropartners.com/meet.

APPENDIX

Image Guidelines

Product Images

We recommend six primary images per product:

1. Main image

    - Use a pure white background.
    - Create a rendering if the product cannot be photographed favorably.
    - Provide product-only shots as well as the product in its packaging. Evaluate which is better.

2. Back of package (if applicable)

    - The image should be highly readable.
    - Good—a photograph of the actual back of the package.
    - Better—a digital export generated from the actual back-of-package label file.
    - Best—content on the back of the package reformatted into a square to maximize online readability.

3. Application shot/lifestyle shot

    - Use an image that shows how the product is used in an ideal use case.
    - Show a person using the product in a relatable way.

4. Features/specifications, key information, infographics

   - Focus on the most important feature/key message.
   - Use large font and not a lot of text so that it's easily readable.

5. Value proposition

   - Use either text or an image to drive home the value proposition.
   - Explain why shoppers should buy from you rather than from the competition.
   - Describe what makes you unique.

6. Either another lifestyle, feature, or value proposition shot

   - Use at least six images for every product.

General image guidelines:

- Images should be high resolution. At least 2,000 × 2,000 or larger (better). Do not resize images down for Amazon.
- White space around products should be trimmed and minimized. Image white space only makes the images appear smaller on the Amazon website.
- Do not add significant product shadow. Do not add a product reflection.
- Regarding the image aspect ratio, the product should be shot naturally, but the area devoted to product images is either square or slightly taller than wide (exact dimensions depend on the page and category). When possible, orient the shot so that the final image is square or portrait.

A+ Images

A+ pages permit five rows of content. The bottom one to two rows should typically be used to feature other products. The first three to four rows should be about the company or the product.

Each of the top three rows can be a single graphic that contains image or text. The goals of the graphics can be to brand, inform, and convert customers. The image size for each row is 970 px × 300 px or 970 px × 600 px.

Please note that there will be a white border around each row.

Here is the basic layout of an A+ page:

Row 1 —970px —300/600px					
Row 2 —970px —300/600px					
Row 3 —970px —300/600px					
Product	Product	Product	Product	Product	Product
Product	Product	Product	Product	Product	Product

Good uses of rows one through three:

- Company branding/messaging
- Product uses, features, and benefits
- Instructions, best practices, examples, and so on

ABOUT THE AUTHOR

Nate Friedman began his e-commerce career in 2014 where he became a top 1 percent seller on Amazon. He has built and managed multiple seven- and eight-figure businesses in the tools, home improvement, kitchen, office products, automotive, and industrial categories on Amazon. Since 2018, Friedman has worked with manufacturers to help them succeed too. He is currently the managing director of Mantaro Partners, an Amazon e-commerce consulting and manufacturing rep firm. Learn more at www.mantaropartners.com.

www.ingramcontent.com/pod-product-compliance
Lightning Source LLC
Chambersburg PA
CBHW021459180326
41458CB00051B/6881/J